D1209842

Creative Therapy 2
Working with Parents

Publisher's Note

This publication is designed to provide accurate and authoritative information in regard to the subject matter covered. It is sold with the understanding that the publisher is not engaged in rendering psychological, medical, or other professional service.

Books in The Practical Therapist Series® *present authoritative answers to the question, "What-do-I-do-now-and-how-do-I-do-it?" in the practice of psychotherapy, bringing the wisdom and experience of expert mentors to the practicing therapist. A book however, is no substitute for thorough professional training and adherence to ethical and legal standards. At minimum:*

- *The practitioner must be qualified to practice psychotherapy.*

- *Clients participate in psychotherapy only with informed consent.*

- *The practitioner must not "guarantee" a specific outcome.*

— Robert E. Alberti, Ph.D., Publisher

Creative Therapy
with
Children & Adolescents
A British Psychological Society Book

Angela Hobday, M. Sc. (Clin. Psych.)
Kate Ollier, M. Psych.

The Practical Therapist Series®

Impact Publishers,® Inc.
ATASCADERO, CALIFORNIA

ATTENTION ORGANIZATIONS AND CORPORATIONS:
This book is available at quantity discounts on bulk purchases for educational, business, or sales promotional use. For further information, please contact Impact Publishers, P.O. Box 6016, Atascadero, CA 93423-6016, Phone: 1-800-246-7228. E-mail: sales@impactpublishers.com

Library of Congress Cataloging-in-Publication Data

Ollier, Kate.
  Creative therapy 2 : working with parents / Kate Ollier, Angela Hobday.
    p. cm. -- (The practical therapist series)
"A British Psychological Society book."
Includes bibliographical references and index.
  ISBN 1-886230-42-0 (alk. paper)
  1. Child psychotherapy. 2. Child psychotherapy--Parent participation.
3. Arts--Therapeutic use. 4. Creation (Literary, artistic, etc.)--Therapeutic use. 5. Parent and child. I. Title: Creative therapy two. II. Hobday, Angela. III. British Psychological Society. IV. Title. V. Series.

  RJ505-C63 H633 2001
  618.92'8914--dc21   2001039201

Impact Publishers and colophon are registered trademarks of Impact Publishers, Inc.

Cover design by Sharon Wood-Schnare, San Luis Obispo, California.
Printed in the United States of America on acid-free paper.
Published by **Impact ✍ Publishers, Inc.**
POST OFFICE BOX 6016
ATASCADERO, CALIFORNIA 93423-6016
www.impactpublishers.com

Contents

Figures

Acknowledgements

Thank you to our families for their ongoing patience and support. Thanks also to Keith Piper for his encouragement, to Val McDermid for her secretarial assistance and to the King's Lynn Psychology Assistants for their administrative support. We are grateful to our trainees, colleagues and the parents on our caseloads who have helped us continue our journeys in creative therapy.

Introduction

Most child therapists love working with children. They enjoy the children's frequent openness and simplicity, and find it easy to create a good rapport, especially with the under-10s. Working with the parents, however, can be less easy, and sometimes really daunting. This is especially true when the parents have been less than understanding or, even worse, abusive towards their child. Therapists may feel a strong loyalty to the child, which if not handled correctly can put them in conflict with the parents. This book aims to help the therapist to feel more at ease in working with parents or caregivers, and to find creative ways of forming a positive working relationship that will ultimately help the child.

Working with children in therapy always involves working with parents, either directly or indirectly. Children are influenced significantly by their parents, especially in the first few years of life. Parents have influenced the child's development and have provided a model for the child in daily activities, problem-solving and dealing with emotions. The emotional and behavioral problems of children develop and are maintained within a family context, which often involves family conflict and parental personality disturbance (Wolff, 1996).

Directly, parents are key people to support children in changing their ways of viewing or dealing with the world. Indirectly, they are also key people in providing an environment that is stable, loving and supportive towards an independent, optimistic future. Thus, when we work with children, we can involve parents both directly and indirectly to promote successful change in the child.

Parents come with their own skills and strengths, maladaptive patterns of behavior and their own needs. What each parent seeks is not always what the child seeks, and the method of reaching these goals may also be different. However, it has been suggested by de Kemp and Van Acker that:

> when the therapist and the parents are... focused on stressing the already present positive moments in the family and on increasing the parents' rearing potentials, a positive outcome can be expected... By emphasizing these abilities, he or she may increase the parents' confidence that they will be able to influence positively the problematic behavior of their daughter or son. (de Kemp and Van Acker, 1997, p. 291).

Our duty as therapists is to learn creative ways of fulfilling the needs of both the child and the parents concurrently.

This book focuses on working creatively with parents to enable the best outcome from behavioral, cognitive or family approaches. There are many published programs dealing with child management, such as *The Parent, Adolescent and Child Training Series* (Herbert, 1996 a,b); and *Early Childhood Parenting Skills: A Program Manual for the Mental Health Professional* (Abidin, 1996). We do not cover that ground within this book. We are more concerned with how to design individual therapeutic programs that include high involvement with the parents. In other words, this book is about the process of working with parents, rather than offering specific "therapies."

❖ *Therapeutic Approach*

In our work as clinical psychologists we tend mainly to use cognitive and/or constructive behavioral approaches. We also use other approaches, such as family therapy, to suit the needs of the child and family. You will find that whenever we give specific guidelines on the approach to be taken, our examples are mainly behavioral. This is to provide a simple basis for illustration and because it is a commonly used approach. Many of the activities are based on family therapy techniques. It is intended that by the time you have read this book you will be able to adapt the material creatively to your own therapeutic orientation.

Respect for clients is essential in any therapeutic situation when you want them to work alongside you. Wise child therapists will include the parents as their clients, not just the child, so that they can extend and utilize the parents' abilities. If they neglect working with the parents, they may well find that all the work they do individually with the child is undermined by an inappropriate or sabotaging parenting style to which the child is exposed, day in and day out. Alternatively, they will lose the child from therapy because the parents see the child becoming too close to the therapist, thus creating a threat to the parents.

Our approach is to take working with parents one step further — to help them become creative and flexible in resolving their child's emotional or behavioral difficulties. We aim to do this by becoming finely attuned to the parents' position, drawing on their skills and building upon them.

❖ *Themes*

As well as increasing creativity in the therapist, there are four main themes running through this book. Each theme relates to our main aim, which is to equip the parents themselves to become the future "therapists" for their children. Our aim is to help them to gain the necessary skills to be able to analyze and resolve many of the emotional difficulties within their family.

The first theme is "parental empowerment." By this we do not mean giving the parent great power over the child, which can place the child in the role of victim. Instead, we want to concentrate on empowering the parent to be a confident, caring person who places the needs of the child first. It is very easy, as professionals, to become "the expert" in clinical settings and take away the power from the parents. We need to recognize that, in most cases, the parents know the child best.

We work on the premise that a parent has the potential to become skilled at being a positive parent, able to meet problems in the child's life and to help the child to deal with them. Obviously, it will occasionally be the case that parents are not able to work within a session with their child, let alone take an active part in promoting change. Sessions with them on their own will help you to determine whether this is something you will be able to help them overcome, or whether their own emotional or mental health needs are such that they require psychological or psychiatric help in their own right.

The second theme is "positive parenting." Our definition of this is similar to that of Sanders et al. (1996 a,b,c,d) who describe it as interaction based on good communication and positive parent attention. They see five important aspects:

- ensuring a safe and interesting environment
- creating a positive learning environment
- using assertive discipline
- having realistic expectations
- parents taking care of themselves as parents.

To promote positive parenting, we aim to equip parents to be rewarders for good behavior, rather than punishers for bad. Where sanctions are necessary, they go hand in hand with rewarding. The use of rewards is elaborated upon in chapter 4, and an information sheet on reward systems is included in Appendix II-9.

The third theme is educating the parents through the creation of information sheets and summary sheets. This book describes how to write easily readable information sheets for parents. We hope the guidelines we give in chapter 3 will help you to create your own information sheets, adapting them to meet the needs and abilities of the clients you have on your caseload. Different ways of presenting information are described, and examples are given.

Having fun is the fourth theme. As in our first title, *Creative Therapy: Activities with Children and Adolescents* (Hobday and Ollier, 1999), our aim is to make sure that therapy is a positive experience for parents, encouraging them to let their ideas flow and be built upon. Some activities for parents to use with their children are included, but it is likely that you will want to create your own because every family is different. Appreciating the parents as very valuable information providers, and building on their strengths, will help to guide them into better parenting practices with minimum resistance and maximum enjoyment.

❖ *How to Use This Book*

This book has been written with the less experienced therapist in mind, although we hope that it includes some ideas and new ways of working which will appeal even to very experienced therapists, and help them to be ever creative. The book draws together many documented sources of information for ensuring good practice as well as including activities and resources that we have developed and found effective in our own practices. There will be something of use to anyone working with parents to overcome children's emotional or behavioral problems, or to promote positive parenting skills.

Most aspects of dealing with parents have been covered in this book. New therapists or those in training may find it helpful to begin by reading right through once and then dipping into it as the need arises. Experienced therapists may wish to use the contents or index to find specific ways to help parents creatively in specific situations.

The information sheets at the back of the book can be used as they are, as resources for parents, but are better used as patterns for creating your own information sheets for the specific clients you have. For example, a teacher may want to adapt some information sheets to meet the special needs of one or two disruptive children in the class — and so may want to introduce some specific guidelines into the "Reward Systems" information sheet (Appendix II-9) which will help to bridge the gap between home and school. The teacher may perhaps wish to add something like: "The star chart can take the form of a book that goes into the school each day so that the teacher may continue to reward for the progress in school."

Consider this book as an aid to being a creative therapist. It does not provide counseling or clinical psychology training in itself. It is full of practical advice and resources for use with a variety of therapeutic approaches that can build on your own training, but is not a substitute for it.

All information sheets and worksheets are copyright free. The rest of the book is subject to the usual copyright restrictions. Where case examples are used, names and some details have been changed to preserve confidentiality.

Creating Rapport

Creating a positive relationship with parents is important if you want them to feel comfortable enough to disclose difficult information to you. Parents also need to listen to you, and to understand your formulation, if they are to engage effectively in their child's therapy. If they feel at ease with you, they are more likely to accept your formulation and think creatively during the session. This will help you to assist them in finding the most suitable and effective means of overcoming the child's difficulties.

A number of studies have demonstrated that a positive relationship which engages the parents as active participants leads to an improved outcome (e.g., de Kemp and Van Acker, 1997; Webster-Stratton, 1998). In fact, some research has suggested that therapist variables may be more important than the therapist's discipline or technical skills (e.g., Pilkonis et al., 1984; Strupp, 1981).

❖ ## Effective Therapists

Although people will vary in their style of interaction with clients, there are common therapist traits which correlate with effectiveness, and undoubtedly help to create a positive working relationship. These include:

— creativity	— analytic thinking
— a sense of humor	— remaining neutral
— credibility	— a high energy level
— enthusiasm	— emotional stability
— self-confidence	— experience in risk-taking
— flexibility	— honesty and compassion
— ability to accept differing beliefs and values	

(Kottler and Brown, 1985; Seligman, 1990).

How the therapist behaves toward parents is also important in promoting a positive outcome. From a variety of research findings (Green and Herget, 1991; Groth-Marnat, 1990; La Greca, 1983; Seligman, 1990) it is possible to put together the following list of factors that can influence the therapeutic relationship significantly:

- offering reassurance and sensitivity to the stress and anxiety that the parents may be experiencing
- offering interventions that are sensitive to the parents' beliefs and values
- supporting and engaging with parents at an emotional level
- communicating an understanding, with interest, respect, warmth and positive regard for the worth of the parents
- self-disclosure and expressiveness appropriate to parents' values
- engaging parents in the therapy process and demonstrating an expectation that parents will take some responsibility for progress
- keeping the focus on track, and giving coherence to the session.

❖ First Impressions

Your first meeting with parents is crucial in creating a positive impression and ensuring that they will return. Your regard for parents and your professionalism start in the setting up of the first appointment. Whether you arrange the first appointment via the telephone and/or by letter, you need to give the parents an idea of how to get to the clinic and what will be involved. Details you may wish to discuss over the phone or send in an information sheet could include:

- date and time of appointment
- where the appointment will be held
- with whom the appointment will be, clearly stating the name and title of the therapist
- who should attend (parents, child, significant others)

- estimated length of appointment — for example, many parents have no idea that psychologists,' social workers' or counselors' appointments last longer than a family doctor's
- how to get there (by car or public transportation) — include a map if it's at all complicated
- details on payment for parking if necessary
- a phone number for them to call if they need to change the appointment time
- a note on confidentiality, stating legal and safety exceptions

Other information may be relevant. Family therapy teams will need to describe the set-up and format of the session.

It is useful to have an information sheet about your service which covers some of the general information from the list above. An information sheet can also let the parent know what the aims of your department are, what sort of difficulties you deal with, whether or not you work with the child alone, the qualifications of the therapists, and the type of therapy you use. This can then be enclosed with the particulars of the appointment. An example of an information sheet about a department can be found in Appendix II-8.

❖ *Creating the Right Atmosphere*

Creating a warm and cozy office conveys a supportive atmosphere and is likely to promote disclosure. Even before you invite the parents into your office there are some factors to think about to set the scene and to help the parents feel at ease. It may help you to walk into your office imagining you are one of your clients. What would be their first impression? If the first thing they see is a pile of files displaying clients' names, they may not have confidence in your ability to keep the session confidential. If your desk is over-cluttered it may give the message that your life is too busy and not ordered enough to have time or energy for them. On the other hand, if your office is too neat and bare they may feel awkward and too formal.

If your room is warm enough (or in hot weather, cool enough) and is made comfortable, then it will help to create a relaxed atmosphere. Use warm, happy pictures on the walls (children's work is fine, but don't have their full name written on them as this will breach confidentiality). Cushions help to make the room look and feel comfortable, and can be useful for the clients to hold or stroke during difficult discussions.

Younger children like to have soft toys around, and often develop a "soft spot" for one or two particular ones in your office. Try to keep your office "toddler friendly' so that you are not having to watch children while interviewing. Lots of activities that are available at floor level can keep most children occupied. On the other hand, many exciting toys that can be seen but are out of reach will cause distractions if the children keep asking for them.

Minimize distractions to demonstrate a commitment to the parents. It is important to divert your telephone calls elsewhere whenever possible. If you must answer the phone, keep it as brief as possible making sure you do not discuss client details.

❖ *Non-Verbal Behavior*

Just as a client's non-verbal behavior provides a great deal of information to you, so your non-verbal behavior indicates the nature and extent of your engagement with your client. Appropriate non-verbal behavior varies according to culture and custom. In the Western world it is generally positive to smile, maintain eye-contact, move your head and change facial expression as you listen, lean forward to show that you are attending to them, and so on.

Where everyone sits in your office also conveys information. It suggests an even power footing if you are able to sit on a seat at the same level as them, but if not, then make clear that you would like to sit on the higher chair. The family's file and some paper left on the chair make the point without having to mention it. If you are on a higher chair, it helps to lean forward to reduce the height difference (and also helps you to look interested).

Showing Respect
❖ ▬▬▬▬▬▬▬▬▬▬▬▬▬▬▬▬▬▬▬▬▬

To establish rapport quickly and easily, it is essential to be seen to be reaching out to the parents. One of the ways of doing this is to walk to meet them from the waiting area, smiling. Speak warmly, in a friendly manner, to invite them into your office. Do not move hurriedly, even if you are running late, as this will give the impression of not having time for them. No matter how busy you have been, parents need to feel that this time is for them, and you need to demonstrate this.

If you have kept the parents waiting, do say "sorry" immediately; you do not have to expand on the reason. Show respect for them as equals.

Be aware of different cultural values, and adapt your manner accordingly. Research has suggested that a therapist's race does not significantly affect treatment outcome (Seligman, 1990), but if the parents have a different ethnic background to you, then it is wise to make yourself aware of what codes of conduct their culture values. For example, Asian families may want you to take off your shoes before entering their home; some religions disapprove of patting children on the head. If you need cultural information, contact any relevant local support center or read up in appropriate literature e.g., McGoldrick et al. (1996). Think creatively about how you can adapt your approach to their different values and beliefs.

Some basic but important skills include:

- On first meeting, introduce yourself and say what they may call you.
- Make sure you get their names right (perhaps clarify that Mom's surname is the same as Dad's, or the pronunciation of a more unusual name).
- If you prefer using first names, then request their permission to do this.
- Make sure you have read their files if they are available. (Not only will a case history be useful to you, but it

also demonstrates to the parents that you are interested in them.)

- If a young child is present with them, get down physically to his or her level and say "hello" to the child using his/her name — be seen to be attempting a special bond with the child.

All this can happen before you have even reached your consulting room or office.

 ## Style

Your style during this initial session is extremely important. Throughout your first session you will be gauging the level at which the parents can understand you and work with you. Be careful to avoid using technical or medical jargon or, if you have to, then be prepared to explain what you mean in lay terms. Make sure they understand your explanations, and pick up on the actual words they use to include in your explanations (Morrison, 1995).

Spending time offering sympathy and concern about the problem and its associated distress can reap numerous benefits. First, it can provide emotional support, which "may provide enormous relief, especially if the patient has felt embarrassed, guilty, or hopeless as is often the case" (Kirk, 1989, p. 15). Morrison (1995) recommends that the early part of the first interview be non-directive "free speech," as this demonstrates that you are interested in what they have to say, and establishes the expectation that parents will take an active role in the therapy. Second, it also gives you important information towards your assessment. You begin to understand the parents' viewpoints and you have an opportunity to see how they work together. Some therapists (for example, Sanders and Dadds, 1993) suggest you do not conduct any formal assessments of parent—child interactions until you have established a trusting relationship with the parents.

Be aware of how you judge your clients. Although none of us operates in a cultural void, it is very important to remember that we all operate according to our own experiences, beliefs, temperament and our own very real fears and anxieties. A rough rule of thumb can be that the "pricklier" the parent, the softer and slower your approach should be. This does not mean that you should condone inappropriate behavior and treatment of the child, but rather you should use positive methods, wherever possible, to achieve behavior change in the parents. If they become angry with you, say that you understand their anger and apologize that what you have said has made them feel this way. Do not retract what you have said if it needs to be said, but certainly say you regret that there is a difference of opinion. Try to return the focus to what you have in common, so that you can build on it.

As you get to know the family, try to include some humor. It boosts everyone's immune system, helps to break down barriers and has been shown to improve therapy outcome (Kottler and Brown, 1985).

Once your relationship has been established, the best way of maintaining it is to keep the parents up to date, give them all the information that they can use, invite their comments, opinions and ideas along the way and treat them as partners and co-therapists in promoting change.

Clear Communication

An easy flow of conversation from the beginning helps to establish clear communication. You may need to break the ice by asking parents about a superficial issue, for example, whether they had trouble finding the place, parking the car, catching the right bus or not getting wet in the rain. If they disclose general information about themselves, such as the sports they play or the music they enjoy, this is good to remember to include in opening conversation in subsequent appointments.

Explain the structure of the session roughly. For example, "During this session we are going to be talking about lots of things, and Sam will also get to do some drawings for me if he wants to. (We don't do doctor's stuff.) First we will have a quick chat together and then I want to see you, Sam, and your parents, separately. And then we'll all get together again and see where we go from here."

Plan to get only two or three ideas/concepts across in any one session. Remember that this is a steep learning curve for parents and we are often asking them to think in ways that are completely foreign to them. You will need to be creative in the way that you describe each concept, which may have to be illustrated in several different ways (see also chapter 3).

❖ *Confidentiality*

This may be a good point at which to discuss confidentiality. If you have sent out an information sheet about your service (e.g., Appendix II-8) before the session, then it may be sufficient to check with the parents that they have read and understood this section. Otherwise you have the more difficult task of explaining that, although you will not be sharing information between parents and children, or telling other professionals all about their personal life, there will be some circumstances where you are legally bound to break the confidentiality. What you actually say could go something like: "What you each say to me is confidential. I will not discuss it with anyone else without your permission. The only exception is if something comes up which has legal implications or if there are concerns for anyone's safety — in which case we shall have to discuss it either together or with other people, but I will ask your permission first." "Ask" is an important word here because at times you may have to divulge information without their permission. For example, if a child or adult discloses that they are suicidal you will have to take steps to ensure they are safe.

Although parents may initially feel anxious about not knowing all that is said during the child-therapist session, they tend to appreciate it in time. You can explain to them that your ultimate aim will be to encourage an open parent-child relationship, so part of your job will be to help the child talk more freely. This can be promoted by encouraging the child to explain to the parents what was done in the child-therapist part of the session. For example, showing Mom his drawing of The Battle (Hobday and Ollier, 1999); showing the stickers he gained for 10 dry nights; reciting the How To Stay Safe rules. When you see the parents after the child's session, you can give general information (and advice) pertaining to the child's progress, or specific information, which has been permitted by the child, that will not jeopardize the confidentiality. Children can be encouraged to let you share some information with their parents if you make it clear that you will not divulge something they are keen to keep to themselves. For example, a girl may be happy for you to let her parents know she is being bullied at school, but not the names of the bullies. Thus, the parents will feel empowered and maintain a sense of keeping up with what is going on. Geldard and Geldard (1997) offer clear advice on dealing with the exclusivity of the child-therapist relationship, and point out that "parents need to have reassurance that in time they will be given all the information that is important for them" (p. 8).

While it is best to see both parents if possible, our experience is that it is often the mothers who take on the role of seeking and attending therapy. Mothers' and fathers' views may differ. For example, mothers tend to report more distress as a result of problems than do fathers (Webster-Stratton, 1990). If parents are separated, it is optimal to invite both parents (at different times) so that you can hear both sides of the story and ensure that no one is feeling left out. Be very clear on confidentiality from the outset, emphasizing that you do not discuss what the other partner has said. Any therapy is best done across both parental settings if possible. The subject of split families is addressed more fully in chapter 6. Our duty, as child or family therapists, is to learn creative ways of fulfilling both children's and their parents' needs concurrently.

❖ *Liaison With Other Professionals*

Liaison with other relevant professionals can be very useful for everyone involved in a case. Such contact can provide you with valuable additional information, perhaps outside your own area of expertise; can minimize replication of services; and allows you to coordinate your work with others towards a more comprehensive outcome. At the same time, liaison can be fraught with ethical dangers. Sattler (1988) reports that malpractice claims often relate to misuse or misinterpretation of assessment information, invasion of privacy and failure to maintain confidentiality.

These risks can be reduced significantly if you keep clients informed, and always seek permission from your clients before contacting schools or other professionals. Many parents are quite happy for therapists working with their children to contact other professionals, but it is still an area that must be treated with caution. Parents can feel very threatened by conversations with other professionals, and this can undermine the kind of working relationship you are endeavoring to achieve.

Any conversations should be reported in full to the parents, and their opinions sought as to the content. If you explain to the other professionals involved that this is going to happen, then you should be able to retain good relationships all around. It is important when sharing information with other systems (e.g., teachers, pediatricians) that you clarify how, when, and with whom your information should be shared — to ensure appropriate confidentiality is maintained, and to make sure that the information will be used most effectively. For example, pediatricians may not find the time to translate your recommendations into appropriate guidelines for nursing staff to follow. Your efforts to provide such guidelines (for the pediatrician to give to the nurses) will increase the chance of nursing staff receiving it, will ensure that you know what the nurses receive, and will allow you to feed back the information more easily to the parents.

Where permission is refused for you to contact the school, etc., then work may have to be done with the parents to help them to realize that they can trust you to use any information wisely. It may be useful to work with them together on what information (such as suggestions on how to help their child) they are willing to have passed on to other professionals.

Keeping the parents informed and in control of how liaison takes place not only minimizes liability, but it can also be an education for parents on how to coordinate different services available to them. Best results are likely to be achieved when you allow the parents to make the decisions. However, there is one important exception — if you consider the child is in danger, then your first duty should be to protect the child. For this you may need to speak freely to the social worker concerned.

2 ❖

Assessment

The main aim of assessment is to analyze the problem situation and work out what is going wrong, and why. Although examining the problems within the family is very important, this phase is also important to establish rapport and to build up a picture of the strengths and dynamics within the family. Remember to spend time feeding back positive affirmations to the parents while gaining information for your assessment, rather than going straight into the treatment phase.

❖ ## The Value of Note-Taking

Taking notes is generally essential during this period as it is impossible to remember all the details, and some that may not seem so relevant at first may be crucial later on. You do not have to write every word verbatim, but your notes generally need to be legible in case, for example, the file goes to court, or someone else takes over the case. It can be useful to read back occasionally, to the parents or child, the last few bits you have written to check that you have got details correct. This serves to give them an idea of the sorts of things you write, and helps to give them more of a sense of control over the interview. It can also add emphasis to something they have told you, helping them to note its importance.

If a parent becomes distressed, it is appropriate to put your file notes aside, reach for the box of tissues, become a listener for a while, and work on the one issue that is upsetting, rather than continuing to follow your line of inquiry. As the parent gains composure, so you can pick up your notes again.

❖ Parents' Expectations

One objective of the assessment is to find out the parents' expectations of treatment, which can be very different from your own. To begin with, parents may have unrealistic beliefs about what constitutes "normal" behavior. They may expect that their child can change "just like that," and may hold the idea that the therapist can "sort the child out," when most situations are more complex and require a broader view and different expectations. It takes skill in questioning, listening and explaining to educate the parents into thinking differently about their child, while at the same time making the parents feel skilled, confident and committed to change. This needs to be based on the positive rapport that you have established.

As you reconcile parents' expectations with your own during the assessment phase, this is also a good time to help them to come to an understanding of their role in helping their own child, and the fact that there is no such thing as a perfect child. Discussing treatment expectations has been found to increase both children's and parents' receptivity to treatment and to alter expectations for therapy outcome (Bonner and Everett, 1986).

❖ Questioning

It is usually most appropriate to ask open-ended questions in order to elicit maximum information. While you are writing down their responses, the parents will have time to come up with further detail, and you have time to think of appropriate follow-up questions. However, be flexible and creative when you are questioning. For example, when the parents go on at a tangent, it may be useful to let them do so (at least for a while). This can give you insight into their style of communicating, their way of perceiving the situation, and can bring out useful information that you may not otherwise have thought of asking about.

There are a number of different types of questions which are valuable when working with parents. If your aim is to pull things apart so that the full nature of the problem is discovered, then it is best to use leading questions and problem definition questions.

With these questions, it is important to adopt the parents' own language. Use their own descriptions and do not simply replace them automatically with descriptions that you prefer. As you listen to parents, you may be reframing their descriptions into your own psychological language, but you must not leap in with your new way of seeing things. Rather, it is best gently to guide and teach them about new ways of perceiving their child — after giving the parents time to feel valued:

> *"If parents really feel the therapist understands and accepts their negative view of their child, they are more than glad to accept the therapist's more positive and hopeful description."* (Rober, 1998, p. 209).

Thus, it is recommended that you demonstrate understanding and acceptance before beginning to "treat" their formulations.

Leading questions can also be used to promote independent thinking in parents. A series of narrowing questions which guide the parents towards logical solutions (Socratic questioning) can help the parents to gain insight and to shift from general abstract ideas to relevant concrete solutions (Stein, 1991). Since it is the parents who make the conclusions, they are more likely to act upon them.

More circular questions can include "behavioral effect" questions, such as "What does she do when she's worried?" and "difference" questions, such as "Who worries the most?" These encourage parents to think about their problem in different ways and can help to bring out patterns and characteristics of family members that they never thought relevant before.

Another type of question involves getting parents to think hypothetically, such as "If you shared your worries with him, what do you imagine he might think?" These can be used to assess the level of understanding a parent has for other members of the family. It can also be used later in the process for planting seeds of ideas.

One study has suggested that circular and reflexive questions may lead to clients feeling more allied with their therapists (Dozier et al., 1998). Hypothetical questions may also be useful where family members experience negativity toward each other, as they remove "emotional investment" (Rueter and Conger, 1995).

❖ *Observation*

In addition to asking family members directly about their current situation, it is very important to observe parents interacting with their children, and with each other. How people perceive themselves may be very different to how you, as a therapist, view them. Observing interactions between family members offers lots of information on how they work together — and can inform you about strengths and needs (of the family) that the family members would never recognize in themselves.

Family activities, such as "Creating cooperation" (Appendix I-4) can be very illuminating, and can provide a fun experience early on which can assist in the development of good rapport. It can be useful to follow the activity by asking each member what they thought their and others' contribution/role was, and then see if this can be generalized to other situations in family life. Be sure to make the activities you use relevant to the topics being addressed in therapy, so that family members do not see them as a waste of time.

Videos can also be very useful for assessing and feeding back the information to family members. However, it is important to remember how powerful such tools can be, and be sure to offer support throughout the process. Knowing some research findings, to put the video in a context, can also help. For instance, if you are getting the family to video their interactions at mealtimes, it will obviously make a difference to the family if they know, before getting feedback, that one such study found the average rate of supportive behaviors to be extremely low (Dadds et al., 1987). Similarly, being aware of typical rates of "parental demands," "non-compliance," "praise" and so on, can be useful to prevent the parents feeling hopeless and helpless.

Information Needed About the Parents

Even if the child is officially your client, you will spend a considerable amount of time using the parents to contribute to the design of the program, and to see it through at home. Some parents will be able to do this easily, while others will not. You may end up working on adjunct issues at the same time to enable them to take their part, such as getting parents to agree on discipline in the home, or improving social support. Therefore, you will need a fair amount of information about the parents themselves. Areas that are often useful to cover are outlined as follows:

Parental Involvement

- How do the parents view their role in intervening with their child?
- To what extent are both parents actively involved?
- What is the quality of the parental relationship? (For example, is there yelling at home? Is there clear and positive communication between family members?)
- How many caregivers are involved with the children?
- What is the level of affection/rejection and warm/aversive interactions with the child? What level and type of social support is used or available to parents, older siblings, extended family or agencies?
- Do the parents share feelings with each other and you?

Parental Style

- What forms of discipline are used?
- What are the definitions or boundaries of acceptable child behavior?
- Do the parents have a passive style (waiting to be told), or do they actively ask questions, read books, etc.?
- What do the parents perceive as strengths regarding their family?
- What ways of dealing with their children have worked best for them?
- Are the parents meeting the child's needs in terms of:

→ offering a close and warm relationship, e.g., through shared activities and interest in the child?

→ a predictable family routine?

→ the use of appropriate contingencies, e.g., homework before play?

→ adequate supervision, e.g., wanting to know where they are?

→ rewarding everyday positive behaviors, e.g., "nice asking"?

→ promoting self esteem and social skills, e.g., recognizing and praising their achievements?

→ a sense of family membership, with shared values and rituals, e.g., having family rules, doing some things together as a family?

→ promoting responsibility and independence?

Parents' Health

- Is there any history of mental illness?
- Have they had any chronic or major acute illnesses?
- Are they currently on medication?

Family Factors

- Who else is in the family (include step-parents, step-children and others)?
- With whom does the child live?
- Is there positive, regular contact for the child with an absent parent?
- What are the current stresses on the family?
- How many times has the family moved (home, school, church, clubs)?
- What are the current living conditions?
- For example, do the children have their own bedrooms? Is money tight?
- What cultural or religious factors may influence family perceptions?

Even though the referral letter to you may clearly state the problem behavior and explain it in a simple manner, it is important that you cover the broad basic information on the child and the family. Often the focus of your therapy may differ from, or be broader than, the referral problem.

Parents' Perception of the Problem

- What do parents see as the problem? Do they differ in their views?
- When did the problem start?
- How did the parents, siblings, school, etc., react to the problem?
- What do they see as the cause of the problem?
- What solutions have been tried, and to what effect?
- How much do they know about the problem? Have they been misinformed? Are there family myths?
- What do they predict for the future regarding this problem?
- Is the child developmentally ready for change?

Information Needed About the Child

Information needed about the child can be gained through the parents and/or the children themselves and may include:

- developmental history
- medical history and present health (any medications or allergies)
- school history, including academic, behavioral and social aspects
- the child's strengths and interests, including hobbies and groups attended
- friendships, both in and out of school
- diet, sleep patterns, daily routines and responsibilities
- any significant events or chronic situations experienced by the child either directly or indirectly.

❖ *Messages to Impart to Parents*

Gaining information from the parents can make them feel cross-examined, and it is normal for them to feel apprehensive and defensive. Your own style during the assessment should be relaxed enough to give the following clear messages to the parents over the first few sessions.

- They are the experts on their child because no one knows them as well as they do.
- There is no "magic wand," but systematically we shall try together to work out what is wrong, and why.
- Progress will take commitment and work from them and from the child.
- Even when the child has been referred, our approach may involve the whole family in helping the child learn new ways of behaving.
- They and the child are not to blame.
- They are extremely important people in helping the child to change.
- Change will not come overnight; it will take time and will need to be worked on in the future to avoid slipping back.
- Stresses on the child or on the family will lead to slipping back into old patterns of behavior (and this is highly likely at some stage!).
- "Slip-backs" (e.g., relapses, reversion to unwanted behaviors) are not disasters, but simply a sign that extra energy needs to go into resolving the problem. We can learn from slip-backs.
- Slip-backs are not anyone's fault. Attaching blame holds us back from finding solutions.
- We usually record what is happening, by using charts, diaries, etc., so we can keep track of progress, and we do not have to rely on our memories regarding how things have been.
- We believe that changes are best made through learning new skills, with activities and rewards along the way — so it is usually good fun.

❖ *Recording*

In these days of clinical evaluation, it is even more important than it used to be to keep records of progress. Keeping a record has a number of important advantages over simply discussing progress:

- It involves parents and children actively in the process of behavior change.
- It offers an accurate, concrete method of measuring change.
- A graphed pre- and post-therapy phase can be a very powerful, motivating, and rewarding experience for both children and their parents.
- It can help to keep relevant family members focused on the target problem.

Recording usually has at least three stages. The first, called the "baseline," records the situation regarding the specific behavior problem before any therapeutic changes are made. The second stage is the "therapy" stage when changes are introduced to improve the problem situation. The third stage, "post-therapy," measures progress once active therapy has finished (although new ways of handling situations may well remain). This final stage allows us to assess whether therapy gains have been maintained over time. These three stages are often followed by further "therapy" and "post-therapy" stages, if the need arises.

❖ *Taking a Baseline*

A baseline is a set of data that is collected before any intervention. It is used to compare pre- and post-therapy behavior, to help to assess whether the program has had the desired effect. It is important because:

- it allows the therapist to see if the target behavior is truly problematic and beyond the norm
- it allows the therapist to see if the target behavior is the right one, for example Tom may be hitting his sister

Sally all the time, but maybe Sally is emotionally terrorizing him

- in a significant number of cases, taking a baseline is sufficient to change the behavior
- it allows the therapist to assist the parents in keeping records reliably, accurately, and at the frequency desired, before intervention begins.

True baseline assessments involve recording what is going on, with no changes in how people are dealing with the situation, and are appropriate for most cases, but not when the following are involved:

- abuse of any sort, including siblings hitting each other to a point of distress
- behavior associated with crisis events
- where life threatening behaviors are involved, such as fire setting.

In order to take a baseline, you will need to establish very clearly with the parents the exact information you wish to record. Use their description of the problem to decide together on the features that will need to be recorded. For example, if a child "goes wild when he doesn't get his own way," you will need to define with the parents the exact nature of his difficulties. "Going wild" may include screaming, biting or hitting and could be redefined as a temper tantrum. The records to be kept could either concentrate on the whole tantrum (looking at its length and intensity) or on a feature of it that the parents particularly dislike, or which causes harm, such as biting.

There are countless ways of measuring behavior. The two most common include 24-hour charts, which focus on frequency of behavior, and ABC charts which look more closely at each incident. 24-hour charts are usually best for high-frequency events, while ABC charts take more time to fill out but offer more in-depth information. It is useful to choose a form of baseline measurement that will also suit the "therapy" and "post-therapy" stages, for ease of monitoring progress.

24-hour Charts

Use a time-linked record, for example a 24-hour chart (Appendix III-1), and write on it the defined behavior. In our example this is "temper tantrums." Together with the parents, work out how it is to be recorded. This will probably include the length of the tantrum and its intensity. Work out with the parents the best way to record this, for example:

- T for tantrum
- Length of tantrum in brackets (5 minutes)
- Major tantrums circled.

An example of a chart completed by parents for a 4-year-old is given in Figure 1. Watch out for this method of recording being too complicated for some parents. If this seems to be the case use a simple "T" for each temper tantrum and perhaps simplify the form to record morning, afternoon and evening (see Split-Day Chart, Appendix III-8).

Figure 1   Sample 24-Hour Chart: Ben's Tantrums

24-Hour Record Chart

Child's name __Ben__   Recorded by __his Mom__

This is a record of __Temper Tantrums__

Date:	Jan. 6	Jan. 7	Jan. 8	Jan. 9	Jan. 10	Jan. 11	Jan. 12
Midnight – 1 am							
1 am – 2 am							
2 am – 3 am							
3 am – 4 am							
4 am – 5 am	T (3)		T (2)				T (2)
5 am – 6 am							
6 am – 7 am		T (2)					
7 am – 8 am			T (4)	T (2)	T (5)	T (8)	T (1)
8 am – 9 am	Ⓣ(2)	T (5)					
9 am – 10 am							
10 am – 11 am	Ⓣ(10) / T (2)	T (3)	Ⓣ(3)				
11 am – 12 noon							
12 noon – 1 pm	Ⓣ(2)	T (2)		T (4)	T (6)	T (3)	T (2)
1 pm – 2 pm							
2 pm – 3 pm							
3 pm – 4 pm	Ⓣ(2)	T (6)	T (3)	T (5)		Ⓣ(4)	
4 pm – 5 pm	T (4)				T (4)		T (2)
5 pm – 6 pm		T (5)	T (15)	T (10)		T (2)	T (2)
6 pm – 7 pm					T (2)		
7 pm – 8 pm	T (10)	Ⓣ(20)	T (5)	T (5)	T (3)	T (3)	
8 pm – 9 pm							
9 pm – 10 pm							
10 pm – 11 pm							
11 pm – **Midnight**							

Please Record   Code

Behavior .... __Tantrum__ .... | T |

Intensity ...... __Major tantrums circled__ .... | Ⓣ |

Other information ... __length in brackets (minutes)__ | (5) |

ABC Charts

An ABC chart is best used when you need detail on each event, for example each tantrum or each bedtime. ABC is short for *antecedent, behavior,* and *consequence* (or before, during and after). It is best to use a chart that explains these terms, so that the parents do not become confused by the three categories. A sample form is given in Appendix III-2. The form takes a measure of what happens before, during and after the event. For illustration, with a tantrum it may be useful to look at what happens just before the event; for example, little brother interrupts play, the activity gets beyond his skill, Mom has just said "No." All of these indicate a reason for the tantrum. Equally, it can be useful to look at what happens after the tantrum, for example little brother cries, Mom becomes angry, Mom gives in. (See Figure 2.)

Changing a child's behavior can be achieved through changing antecedents and/or consequences. Antecedents can also involve predisposing factors and a broader context, such as established household rules, skills to recognize when to ask for help, skills to "reframe" frustrations. Consequences can also involve the long term and might include saving money toward a goal, or acting up at school until suspended.

Which aspects you record on the ABC chart will depend on the problem situation. The more detailed a picture the parents can offer, the more able you are to establish the importance of place, time, which friends, which part of the week, and so on. More details on ABC charts can be found in Herbert (1987, 1996 a,b).

It is generally useful for the child to bring the charts to each session for review, and you should keep a copy for the file. As the information mounts, it is often useful to make a simplified frequency chart or graph (over time) so that the family can gain a snapshot of progress. It can help to use a bar chart or graph where the vertical axis is well exaggerated so that small gains will be easy to see, as in Figure 3. (see page 31)

Figure 2   Sample ABC Chart: Tom's Tantrums

ABC Record Chart

Child's name ___Tom___   Recorded by ___Jennifer (mother)___

This is a record of ___Tom's temper tantrums, especially with Simon___

Date	Time	Antecedents What happened before?	Behavior Describe the actual behavior	Consequences What happened next?
Jan 2	10:30	Simon crawled over Tom's Lego™.	Tom had a tantrum. He smacked Simon's arm & yelled & threw his Lego™ around for 20 seconds.	Simon cried. I rescued Simon & yelled at Tom.
Jan. 16	2:00	Simon crawled towards Tom's Lego™.	Tom brought Simon to me.	I thanked Tom for bringing Simon to me. Cuddled Simon while Tom showed me what he had made.

Figure 3   Sample Bar Chart: Sam's Progress

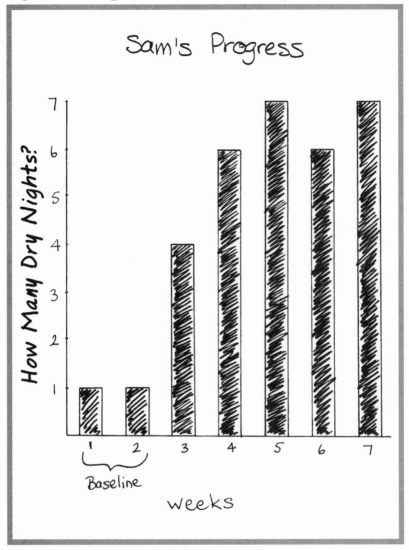

Recording progress before and after treatment, in a way that is easily understood, will help the parents to keep motivated. It will also help everyone pick up on any small gains which may otherwise go unnoticed. For further information on recording progress, see pages 57-59.

3 ❖

Sharing Information

❖ *Verbal Information*

Information is remembered most clearly when the main message is said at the beginning and then again at the end, with the explanation or illustrations in the middle. Remember that what may seem obvious to us as experienced therapists may be a revelation to most parents. Thus, our explanations have to be clear and simplified as much as possible, according to the parental level of understanding. The amount of information given to parents at any one session needs to be limited to give them time to assimilate it into their own knowledge and conceptualization.

The main message of a session may need to be repeated a number of times in different ways so that the listener has numerous opportunities to make sense of the information. Throughout your sessions, it can be useful to encourage the parents to discuss their understanding of the situation so that you can check that they are on the same "wavelength" as you. When they are not, try to establish some common ground and move forward from there. For example "we've looked at your strategies so far and you have discovered that Jenny is calmer when she has plenty of sleep. This is why it seems like a good idea to start working on her sleep first to help her overcome her tantrums. What do you think?"

Judge carefully the amount of information that a parent can cope with at each session and tailor it to the parent's intellectual level and emotional state. Many parents cope best with "bite-sized" chunks of information. Webster-Stratton (1992 b) has suggested the idea of refrigerator notes: as part of a structured

33

package she produced standard notes which the parent then attached to the fridge as a reminder. With individually tailored therapy plans, it is useful to compile some very brief summary notes together at the end of a session for the parents to pin up somewhere. Keep the notes brief, and even coded if the child is likely to quote the note back. For example, if an argumentative child sees Mom's note to herself "Don't argue back" and then Mom does, the child is likely to say "You know you aren't allowed to argue with me any more."

❖ Using Research

It is useful if you have access to some research related to the issue. Although this may not be needed, in some cases it can help in the following ways:

- To give credibility — for example, if parents have trouble giving up the idea of punishment to carry out the suggested changes in antecedents.
- It adds professionalism to your work — you are able to show the parents that you know what you are doing.
- It can help to put their troubles into perspective, e.g., 10 to 15 per cent of school children have stomach pains at some time (Sanders et al., 1990) — they are not alone.
- Seeing research results can give both children and parents positive expectations regarding their problems.
- Seeing positive results in research motivates both children and parents in working on the program.

Always remember to use research findings carefully. When you are working with parents to help them to be more creative in their thinking about their own child, the research is only a tool to assist them and you. There is the danger that you can "pull rank" over the parents by finding research to back up your ideas, thus ruining the collaborative relationship that you are seeking to establish.

A word of warning: scientific facts last only so many years before they are taken over by new facts, philosophies, and trends. Thus, there is no absolute truth in most of what is written, although we are probably approaching truth. So it is best to discuss research in terms of what the findings "suggest and indicate," rather than as absolute facts.

❖ *Explaining Our Perception*

When being introduced to a new concept in relation to their child or family, parents may have problems relating general ideas to their own situation. It is very important to help the parents to accommodate the new concept, and its relevance, into their own way of thinking, through discussion with you along the way. Explaining how a concept fits might relate to the criteria for diagnosis or the analysis of the baseline. Alternatively, it may be more to do with the family history, patterns of behavior, or some other factor that has come to light during your first interview.

It is important that parents consider what this means for the child. For example, maybe the child has problems in understanding more than one instruction at a time, or they may have problems understanding how their behavior impacts others. Alternatively, the child may need to learn other ways of getting the attention they need.

❖ *Therapy — A Lifestyle Decision*

Parents need to become informed about what this means for themselves. For example, there may be a need to change the style of consequences and antecedents, implement changes in the family routine, establish clear family rules, work on ways to praise, be involved in associations or organizing respite care. Webster-Stratton, in her work with parents of early-intervention children, found that active participation may lead to "more self-confidence, increased internal control, increased self-esteem, increased community involvement and decreased isolation" (Webster-Stratton, 1998, p. 716).

The parents need to be aware of what is involved in setting up a therapeutic program. For example, it may involve having to record at home, practicing new ways of making requests (see

Requests, Appendix I-9), keeping in communication with the teacher, keeping monitoring forms on the bedroom wall, involving all the children in using a chores chart, visiting the therapist, spending money on rewards. A program needs to be suited to the parents' emotional and financial resources.

❖ *Visual Information*

All verbal information is best remembered if backed up with visual information as well. Thus, videos, drawings and information sheets are invaluable tools in educating parents. These allow the parents to go over the information in their own time, for clarification and reminding. Putting information sheets and drawings in a prominent position in the home can act as a cue to the parents to think about their own behavior in relation to the problems they are working on. It is also useful for parents to be able to reacquaint themselves with the information when, perhaps years down the track, a similar problem resurfaces.

Do not be afraid to draw sketches or Likert scales to illustrate your information, or to gain information from a parent. A Likert scale gives a linear measurement of a problem. For example, you may wish to draw a line on a piece of paper and ask the parents something like "Where do you see Jo's moodiness now if this end of the line is no moods and this end is moody all the time?" This sort of approach can lead to a discussion about where a 12-year-old's level of moodiness might be acceptable (see Figure 4). Such scales can also be used repeatedly over the course of therapy to monitor progress.

Figure 4   Sample Likert Scale: Jo's Moods

1	2	3	4	5	6	⑦	8	9	10
Not moody			Acceptable level						Moody all the time

Diagrams may also be needed to demonstrate symptoms, such as the areas of the body affected by anxiety. Encourage parents to link this up to be relevant to their own child by drawing on their own knowledge and observations.

❖ *Giving Written Information*

Information sheets are very useful for parents to take away so that they can remember all the details you have given them. They are more than "handouts" because, as we use them, they are not simply handed to the client. We have found they are best used within the sessions and then given to the client to take home. In that way you will know that the information has been given at least once (in your sessions) even if the parents never read it. If you have been able to discuss the contents, you will be sure that the information given has been understood and interpreted in the right way. The parents are also more likely to keep referring to the information sheet if they feel they already have some knowledge and understanding of the subject matter. It promotes the sharing of the therapy that you are trying to establish. Something you have discussed together, with some helpful notes to take home, is better than being handed a sheet of information by a therapist who seems to know it all.

As well as serving as a long-term reminder, information sheets are a useful way to involve the other parent if they do not come to the sessions. If the information given on the sheets has been discussed thoroughly in the sessions, then it is easier for the attending parent to pass on the information to the non-attender. If used for this purpose, it is usually a good idea to make the information sheets quite detailed.

If you are intending to use information sheets that have been prepared by someone else, make sure you have read them through first and agree with everything on them. (This applies even to the information sheets within this book!) If you have to give out information sheets with the proviso "Of course, I don't quite agree with everything there," then the whole sheet is liable to be ignored.

Designing Information Sheets
The following guidelines will help you to write useful information sheets:

a) Readability

Creating easily readable information sheets is essential. If they are too difficult to read they are likely to end up in the trash or at the back of a drawer. Despite many formulae being available for checking readability and comprehensibility, recent studies continue to find a gap between the reading ability of patients and families, and the reading difficulty of the material (for example, Le Bas, 1989; Meade and Smith, 1991; Reed et al., 1993; Singh, 1995). The language used should be clear, but not patronizing. Short sentences in short paragraphs work best, or numbering points down a page as in "Helping your child to follow requests" (Appendix II-6).

It is sometimes difficult to work out whether the language you have used is easy enough for most of your clientele to understand. Back in 1948, Flesch devised the Reading Ease Formula, which is still in common use today. Basically, this is a way of working out the average number of syllables per 100 words by counting the number of syllables in the passage selected. Once the length of sentences is calculated, a reading ease score can be worked out which can indicate the percentage of the population who would understand the text (Ley, 1973). Others have also developed readability scales (Sawyer, 1991), and a number of computer software programs have been developed (for example, Harrison and Bakker, 1998; Peterson et al., 1992) which may be useful for those who wish to pursue the subject further.

An alternative way of developing information sheets that can be used by the majority of your clientele is to only use vocabulary from a children's dictionary. An example of a suitable dictionary would be *D K Merriam-Webster's Children's Dictionary*. Another recommendation taken from a study on readability of consent forms (Peterson et al., 1992) is to use graphics and "simple declarative statements as headings for each paragraph" (p. 6). An example of an information sheet with simple statements as headings is given in "Helping Your Child to Follow Requests" (Appendix II-6).

Sticking to the vocabulary in a children's dictionary may not be completely possible, because you will probably need to include some medical or psychological terms. However, it will give you a rough guide. Remember to keep sentences short and simple.

If all this sounds very complicated, you may choose instead to design two levels of information sheet on each of your topic areas. One would contain a lot of information and use a more complicated vocabulary. The other would be far simpler and suitable for those with less comprehensive literacy skills. The latter may benefit from the use of illustrations to supplement the text, as mentioned above. For an example of two different ways to present similar information, compare "Helping Your Child to Become Less Anxious" (Appendix II-4) and "Helping the Child Who Worries Too Much" (Appendix II-7). The second information sheet will be easily read by a much larger proportion of the population.

b) Style

The information sheets you write need to be non-sexist unless you are writing different texts for boys and girls. The English language is rather cumbersome when it comes to using both male and female genders, resulting in the use of "his or her" and "s/he," which may interrupt the flow of your text. You may find it easier to be less grammatically correct and use "their" or "they," even for a single person, such as "Your child may want their friends to play."* Another way to get around the problem is to put an explanation at the beginning

---

*Editor's note to the U.S. edition: The authors have identified and responded well to a thorny problem in contemporary English usage. None of us wants to slight either gender, but our pronouns are often not up to the task. Nonetheless, the editor at Impact Publishers remains a traditionalist when it comes to agreement of subject and pronoun. "A person" (singular) is never "they" (plural). With sensitivity to the matter, it's not terribly difficult to rewrite a sentence or paragraph to (a) make it gender neutral, or (b) make a reference plural (e.g., "children" rather than "child"), so "they" works, or (c) make up an example using a gender-specific name, so the use of "she" or "he" becomes appropriate. (This latter approach often makes your point most clearly anyway.) In longer works, it's possible to alternate female and male examples throughout, so both genders are roughly equally represented. — REA

along the lines of "Throughout this leaflet we have referred to girls, for ease of reading. Please read it to include boys." You would be wise to use whichever gender is most appropriate for the subject you are discussing. For example, there are more girls with eating disorders (Lask and Bryant-Waugh, 1993), so an information sheet about these would be more appropriately aimed at the parents of girls.

In most cases, watch out for cultural overtones and try to eliminate these. For example, suggested activities may need to include those that cross cultural boundaries. Be sensitive to your locality and design your information sheets with your clientele in mind. A helpful rule is to think of your most "different" parents, whether in lifestyle, culture or attitude, and try to work out what objections they would have to your information sheet.

If you are writing for parents with special needs, for example those with learning difficulties, take advice from others who work with that client group to check whether your level of information is appropriate for them.

c) *Content*

The subject matter of your information sheets will obviously depend on what you are aiming to teach the parents. Some examples are given in the Appendices at the end of this book. All of these have been piloted by being used with parents in this, or a similar form, with the request that the parents tell us about anything they have found difficult to understand or that is unclear.

When you are planning your content, think about the aim and scope of the information sheet, then jot down the main facts you wish the parents to learn. Check any content about which you are unsure by looking it up in a mainstream text. Check any quotes or references. Be careful not to write an information sheet for the wrong reason, for example, because it looks like a more official way of getting over your own unorthodox view. If it is ground-breaking stuff which you are sure the parent needs to know, make it clear that it is "all your own work" and float it past your colleagues first, to make sure you are not way out of line. As a general rule, it is best to save these new ideas for presentations to other professionals or for journal articles.

d) *Presentation*

The same information can be presented in many different ways. One helpful way is in the form of questions that are answered. Examples of this are "Reward Systems — Some Questions Answered" (Appendix II-9) and "When a Parent Goes Away" (Appendix II-11). When creating your own information sheets think about the questions you are often asked on that particular subject. You will need to include some very basic information. Do not assume that something obvious is too obvious to put in the information sheet. Not all parents have the same knowledge, and people are quite accepting of very basic information if it is on a standard information sheet.

Information can be presented in short paragraphs under suitable headings. Another way of presenting the information is through using "bullet points" or numbers. There are several information sheets in this style that we have included in the Appendices. Sometimes it is appropriate to include several different styles in one information sheet so that information is broken up visually (see "Helping Your Child to Become Less Anxious," Appendix II-4). Information sheets are best kept short. Two sides of a well-spaced 8½ x 11" piece of paper is usually the longest we would expect to use. Some therapists find it useful to have very small fact-sheets in a series, which build up as the sessions proceed. This is a useful way of helping the parents to digest small amounts of information at a time.

e) *Creating Individual Information Sheets*

Information sheets can be targeted towards specific groups or individuals. An example for groups would be our nearly identical information for parents of children in split family situations. There is one for fathers and one for mothers

(Appendices II-2 and II-3). If they are targeted towards individuals, it is useful to keep a standard information sheet on a computer disk and to tailor it as appropriate. This can then emphasize the main points you have discussed within the session.

f) *Summary Sheets*

One step beyond information sheets is the individual summary of the session (referred to earlier in this chapter under "Verbal Information"). Summarizing the session in written form, and giving it to the parent will help to consolidate the progress made and encourage the parent to keep to the plan you have devised together. Do not forget to include the parent's ideas and write the summary in a way that indicates a partnership in the therapy. For example, ask the parent to write it and suggest that they write something like "This week I have decided to: ...." This will make it seem more personal and more as if the parent "owns" the ideas than if you were to write "This week you will do the following: ...." If the summary is written in a very concise way, on an index card, it is more likely to be put up on the fridge or bulletin board as a reminder. Writing it out by hand in the session will not look as business-like as preparing it on the computer, but it has the great advantage of being immediately available to take home and the parents can write it themselves.

At the very end of therapy, a summary letter can be written to the parents outlining the progress made (see "Closure" in chapter 5). This can serve as a useful reminder if the problems reoccur and they need to remember how they helped their child to resolve them.

Handouts That the Parents Bring to the Session

From time to time you will find that a parent brings a standard handout from elsewhere to your session, saying they have found out what is wrong with their child. (Currently, more often than not, it relates to attention deficit disorder!) This is where you will really have to remember you are trying to work in partnership with the parents and equip them to help their children. Never dismiss the leaflet with a few words, especially if the words you choose show you are pulling rank. An example of this would be "Oh yes, well of course I am *quite* aware of the symptoms of ADHD as set out in *DSM IV* and I can assure you that your child does not fall into that diagnostic category." Instead, go through the leaflet carefully with them, and perhaps compare other diagnoses to help them come to their own conclusion about how complicated making a diagnosis really is. Make comments about detective work, and it being useful to look at the problem from all angles. If they are still convinced they have it right, help them to accept that whatever the diagnosis, their child will benefit from the therapy plan you have begun to use.

Most parents will accept your opinion, or agree to differ, but in any case try out the plan you have devised together. However, if they are really set on the idea that there is something else wrong with their child you may need to follow this through. In this case, refer them for a second opinion to someone you can trust to do a thorough diagnostic interview. After all, you may just be wrong and the parents deserve to be heard. However, bear in mind the barriers to progress outlined in chapter 5.

❖ *Giving Bad News*

Having to inform the parents of "bad news" regarding their child can be difficult. The news can be received either positively (for example, relief, if the parents suspected it all along) or as a dreadful grief-stricken shock (for example, if the child has just revealed suicidal ideation or that they were abused).

Three important points to remember are:

1. You have to tell them as soon as is realistically possible, as they have the right to know.

2. You should provide further information, again as soon as possible, regarding the news, in terms of therapeutic or clinical information that will help the parents to understand, and also prevent them from catastrophizing.

3. It is useful to explain how the parents can help the situation, and you should give them written information on this before they leave, even if only roughly written notes.

Being told bad news disempowers parents and research indicates that often the content of the session will not be remembered (for example, Green and Murton, 1993). Parents need to build up a sense of control and constructive attributions. Even if the parents' behavior may have contributed to the bad news (for example, neglect led to abuse by others), it is more constructive to focus on what they can now do to improve the situation, such as "we would all do things differently if we had a second chance, but what is important now is to find the best way to move forward. You are committed to helping your child, and that is really good. We can work together to help you to be able to help her in the best way possible."

Parents should leave your session with some constructive, practical written information that they can read over in their own time. This will allow them to absorb the information in a calmer state of mind.

❖ *Writing Reports*

Communicating results to others is an important skill for therapists to master. Reports generally need to be written to the referring agent, for court cases, and to other professionals with whom you are liaising. Each will take on a different form in order to be meaningful and useful to the reader, while not threatening the confidentiality and possibly vulnerable status of your client.

While writing style is an individual matter, in general it is useful to follow the guidelines below:

- Write to suit your readers. Work out what they want and need to know, with due regard for the understanding and qualifications of the recipient.
- Use varying lengths of sentences, but don't let them get too long or complex.
- Keep paragraphs shorter rather than longer.
- Use headings, where necessary, to make your points clear.
- Avoid jargon wherever possible. Sattler (1988) reports that even psychologists, teachers, and psychiatrists disagree on the interpretation of psychological terminology.
- Use clear, simplified language — use a clinician's guide if necessary (e.g., Gowers, 1973; Zuckerman, 1993).
- Keep the style logical, concise and precise, using examples to support your inferences and conclusions.
- Draw your conclusions and inferences cautiously and link them closely to the information presented.
- Any test results should be presented with interpretive explanations.
- The length of your report needs to suit the reader.
- For example, if it is a report to a family doctor who referred the child, one page is all they are likely to have time to read.

Confidentiality is a major issue with written reports that may be read by others. It is good practice to ask permission from the parents about sending copies of reports to other professionals concerned with their child. If you are able to explain that this is in the best interests of their child, most parents will agree.

However, they may wish to know what you are likely to say. As always, if the child is at risk, your obligation is to inform other relevant professions with or without the parents' permission.

When you write your report, be sure to specify to whom the report is intended, with appropriate statements across the top of pages relating to confidentiality. Where possible, exclude material that would severely damage your relationship with the parents. If you must convey such information, this may be better done orally at a time when you can give full consideration to the issues at hand. A good rule is to imagine that the parents have access to your letter or report (as indeed they may in the future). This will help you to check your words carefully, remembering to respect your clients.

An initial letter to the referring agent is one common report required when working with families. This is usually written after one or two appointments, after a formulation and hypothesis have been generated. The content generally includes:

1. Identifying information.
2. Details of where and when you have seen the family to date.
3. A summary of your assessment.
4. Observations and clinical impressions, along with any formal test results.
5. An explanation of what you think is happening, which includes your formulation and hypothesis (see "Planning Together" in chapter 4).
6. Recommendations and current plan of action.
7. Expected length of therapy or when you are likely to write next.
8. Close with signature over your title.
9. On the bottom, a note of who else will be sent a copy of the report.

Summary updates should be sent occasionally to the referring agent, and to any other professional with whom you have been liaising, to keep them informed. When you have finished therapy, it is appropriate to write to all the professionals with whom you have liaised, to inform them that your client has been discharged.

4

Making Progress: Developing a Plan

❖ *Planning Together*

The therapeutic process tends to follow a set sequence of stages, each of which can actively involve parents.

1. Further assessment, as a joint process, of the child's situation and of the family processes, e.g., baseline, skill level, family perceptions.
2. Float hypotheses by working together to find patterns on the information gathered.
3. Create a formulation, based on the parent's ideas, to explain the problem situation. The simplest way to do this is by writing the "story" together about what has happened and why, and including the cause of the problem.
4. Generate a positive program plan to change the situation, based on the parent's choices. This may include one or more interventions and involve one or more people (see "Encouraging Change," Appendix I-5).
5. The parents and the child need to choose appropriate rewards to be used, and decide when and how they will be used. It is important to remember that rewards need to be based on the child's likes (see "Reward Systems," Appendix II-9).
6. Introduce the interventions as a joint exercise, with the parents, child and yourself, using large amounts of praise along with the chosen rewards.

7. Encourage parents to monitor progress using star charts, record forms and pictures. Monitor progress yourself through phone calls and clinic sessions.

8. Review progress together, which will lead to changes along the way to "fine tune" the program, and provide the opportunity to hand over more and more responsibility to the parents.

9. Plan for closure so that the parents are willing and able to become independent in managing family problems (see "Closure" in chapter 5).

❖ *Joint Approach*

Keeping parents (as well as the child) involved, and a part of the planning process, has many benefits in maintaining communication and empowering the parents (Davies, 1993). It is also more likely that therapy will be successful if parents are involved. For example, Newby (1996) and Young et al. (1995) found parental involvement can lead to the following positive gains:

- It builds up parents' knowledge base.
- It builds parent-child rapport because they are working together.
- It enhances parents' attending skills.
- It teaches parents a problem-solving approach (for more information on teaching problem-solving, see D'Zurilla and Nezu, 1982; Forgatch and Patterson, 1989; Spivack et al., 1976).
- It teaches the parents formal behavior modification that can be generalized.
- It promotes informal social reinforcement. It teaches alternatives to any inappropriate methods that parents have been using.

As each family differs, so too must our style and level of engagement with them. More competent and insightful parents are likely to fare better with an active therapeutic role, while families that have significant disturbances may have more success with the therapist holding more power and sharing less (Hampson and Beavers, 1996). Assessment should clarify to what extent each family member can manage involvement throughout the therapeutic process.

So, too, our focus must remain broad. Therapy programs can fail because they do not address parents' negative communication patterns, anger management problems and poor problem-solving abilities (Webster-Stratton, 1994), which may go hand in hand. For example, a family's ability to problem-solve successfully is reduced if family members engage in hostile and conflicting interactions (Rueter and Conger, 1995). The therapist can gain insight into the dynamics of the family through observing how family members problem-solve together.

❖ *Building Blocks to Therapy*

In the majority of cases, we are seeking to empower parents and to give them the skills to be able to work independently at problem-solving and problem resolution, using positive practices based on a greater understanding of why the problem has arisen in the first place. In order to do this, we recommend three steps.

1. *Build up family cohesion*

The first step aims at promoting a positive outlook and perception of the family as a whole. It takes the focus away from the "problem child" and the family hassles, and instead has the family being motivated to work together as a team. Make the family aware of its skills, knowledge and values "as a family." Activities such as "Combined Strengths and Skills" (see Appendix I-3) help the family to focus on their assets, rather than on their problems. An example is provided in Figure 5. Help the children to feel valued rather than just a source of problems (see "Helping Your Child to Feel Valued," Appendix II-5). Promote cooperation between family members (see "Creating Cooperation," Appendix I-4), and promote communication between family members (see "Balanced Messages," Appendix I-2; "Requests," Appendix I-9). Work on the family doing things together and working towards a (non-problem related) goal. Some family problems will improve simply with a change of focus on to the positive. At every stage, explain to the family why they are doing a particular task, and after each activity, link it back to the aims of the therapy. Otherwise they will think they are wasting their time coming to the session to "play family games."

Figure 5   Sample Combined Strength and Skills

good listener
loving
practical
good at Math

good at discipline
(usually)

loving toward my children
good cook
creative
caring

good football player
patient
good with money

logical

good with washing,
ironing etc.

tidy

sense of humor

helpful with housework

2. Introduce skills and knowledge by building on the family's base
Start simple and work up, so that the family keep up and gain confidence. It is important to use hypothetical examples at this stage, so that the practice remains emotionally neutral. Examples of skills to teach include:

- data recording
- further communication skills, such as learning to say "I feel let down when you do X" rather than "you stupid idiot… when will you learn?"
- analysis skills, such as looking for the pattern in the ABC learning about more distant antecedents and consequences through case examples
- problem-solving with written-up (hypothetical) problems.

Make sure you offer sufficient support when working with families that exhibit a hostile interaction style, as this is predictive of destructive problem-solving behavior and reduced effectiveness (Rueter and Conger, 1995). It has been suggested that working on hypothetical problems can assist in reaching agreeable solutions without negativity. This is especially true when, for example, an aggressive adolescent is involved (McColloch et al., 1990). Hypothetical cases are also useful if people tend to go off on tangents, have an inflexible approach, or belittle other family members. This is because there is no emotional investment in a hypothetical case, and they can be used as demonstrations of the power of family cooperation.

3. Introduce problems relating to the family
Again, it is important to start small, so that the family succeeds in its early attempts to problem-solve its own situations. Support family members (without doing it for them) to problem-solve one problem at a time — although the parents may realize that one antecedent or consequence may lead to many problems, or may resolve lots of problems.

It may require a careful balance in your sessions, as to how much you introduce in any one session, so that the parents feel they are "moving" in the therapy rather than "going back to school" by learning theory. Making activities fun and creative helps them to feel they are gaining from such exercises, and helps link theory to practice. Information sheets can be used to back up the therapy, for example, a summary on dealing with aggressive behavior in teenagers (see Appendix II-1).

Research has suggested that parents who behave in a negative manner toward their children tend to continue to do so and demonstrate poor problem-solving abilities (e.g., Rueter and Conger, 1995). Thus, where negativity exists, we as therapists need to train the parents in ways to perceive problems (see "Family Needs," Appendix I-6), generate solutions, and apply positive changes. Enabling parents (and their children) to be competent in these skills helps them to participate in the development of a therapy plan.

❖ *Designing an Individual Therapy Plan*

Individual programs vary enormously in order to cater to the needs of the child, parents and family situation. They can range from enabling parents to carry out simple contingency management to complete involvement of parents as co-therapists in assessment, planning, implementation and generalization (Herbert, 1991). Although we favor a "Partnership Model" (Davies, 1993), the level of parental involvement will depend on their skills and needs at the time.

While the therapist is the facilitator in this process, it is important that the parents and child take a full and active role in choosing which aspects of the problem should be measured, targeted and changed. They can also discuss and choose the most appropriate fun ways to measure progress. See if you can encourage a parent to summarize the discussion; for example, Mom's summary may go along the following lines: "We've decided that at the end of each day Tom needs to talk to someone about his practice that day, how it went. OK, so Tom will talk to Dad each night after his bath about the practice. Now, one of us needs to keep a record, so I can do that. How about Tom lets me know that you two have discussed Tom's progress, so that I can write it down to bring back to the sessions?"

❖ *Content of an Individual Therapy Plan*

A vast number of variables have been studied regarding their impact on therapy. More general guidelines that can be incorporated into most programs, and which may promote smooth progress include:

Start simple

Start with a simple focus while the child and parents begin to understand the ideas presented and discussed.

Be flexible

Parents' views on the formulation will sometimes differ from yours. In order to maintain alliance, it is best to present the program (when possible) as based on their formulation, so that parents will perceive the program as a product of their efforts, and will be motivated to carry it through. Focusing on a dispute in formulation will only damage the relationship, and is unnecessary if it is possible to create positive change without getting parents offside. If no change happens with the plan that follows from their formulations, help them to look again at their understanding of the causes.

Start small

Break the major goal into many small ones, and make sure the first can be easily achieved to increase motivation and positive expectations, for both children and parents. Parents are more likely to work for goals that they perceive as achievable through personal effort (Lefcourt, 1976).

Define clearly

Be clear and agree on what problem is being worked upon, and define acceptable performance. Avoid "fuzzy" descriptions, for example, "often soggy at night" can be made clear as "has three wet beds per week."

Prepare for slip-backs

Discuss "gray areas" in the session to help clarify the main criteria involved. Make sure that the parents understand that very often the targeted behavior gets worse before it gets better. This is because of the child's need to recreate familiar patterns. The aim of therapy is to create new positive patterns. A parent's inability to understand the reasons for the behavior worsening is a common cause of failure in therapy.

Close initial contact

Involve frequent contact with the parents in the early stages to troubleshoot as necessary, to maintain enthusiasm and to reward all participants for their efforts.

Generalize

Include generalization as part of the plan to assist therapy gains to maintain in different situations (Sanders and Dadds, 1993).

Be positive

Focus on building positive skills rather than on punishing. Encourage parents and children to talk to each other (see "Ten Ways to Help Your Child Talk to You," Appendix II-10). Introduce positive consequences for a move in the right direction. Encourage parents to demonstrate warmth to their children, as this has consistently been found to improve a child's social competence, problem-solving effectiveness, etc. (Putallaz and Heflin, 1990; Rueter and Conger, 1995).

Broaden the focus

Incorporate other aspects of family functioning, such as mealtimes, and promote positive skills, such as listening to children. These will improve progress and help prevent old patterns from re-emerging. For example, it may help a child to attend a social skills group, as well as having a parent and child individual program.

Education

Include education for the child (depending on age) and the parents. Even 2- or 3-year-olds can learn the rules about inappropriate behavior if these are kept simple and well illustrated, for example, with puppets.

Context

Be sensitive to the parents' and child's position and other factors going on around them. Marital problems, for example, are known to impact on children's behaviors.

Marital therapy

Incorporate marital therapy if it appears appropriate. If the parents are unwilling to address this separately, try to introduce it informally. For example, suggest that Dad ask Mom "How was your day," and "What can I do to help?" when he gets home. See also the section on "marital discord" in chapter 5 (pages 63-64).

The right level

Discuss all aspects of the program to ensure you have adapted the level of complexity to suit the parents and child. This should not be a problem if the parents have taken part in the design of the program.

Developmentally appropriate

Help the parents to come up with developmentally appropriate levels of responsibility for the child's program. For example, 12-year-old children can usually manage themselves. When parents are aware of the level of their child's thinking it tends also to promote the child's self-regulated problem-solving (Shumow, 1998).

Incorporate research

Be up to date with research that suggests a preferred mode or style of therapy; for example, younger children respond to simpler approaches that involve them directly as well as their parents, such as a personalized behavioral program.

Optimism

Create a sense of optimism by recognizing small gains, and the use of cognitive techniques.

Promote lifestyle

Encourage the parents to incorporate aspects of lifestyle if it seems lacking. For example, incorporated in your approach may be family outings or meals together.

Build strengths

Build up the child's strengths in other areas as well as targeting the problem behavior. Getting rid of the problem might not gain status, but being particularly good at something will. With the parents also, build up their strengths and promote the use of praise (see "Many Ways to Praise," Appendix I-8, and "What Behaviors Can We Praise?" Appendix I-11).

Family balance

Be aware of the family dynamics. Any changes in the way people act towards each other can affect the family balance (Burnham, 1988). For example, when the parents focus on the difficulties of one child, it may create more problems for another (see chapter 5, p. 63).

Promote independence

Remember, you are aiming to help the family to become independent of you. The more you can give them control over the program, the more easily they will tackle a future problem in the same way.

❖ *Monitoring Progress*

Progress on a program needs to be monitored and evaluated on a regular basis to pick up any problems as they arise, and to maintain a focus on the changes sought. Monitoring is usually in the form of progress sheets kept at home, together with contact with the therapist. Although therapists tend to take monitoring forms for granted as part of a program, they can be a whole new adventure for families, so education in record keeping is important. Some tips to promote the family understanding of record keeping include:

- Explain why record charts are necessary and why it is useful for the whole family to be involved.

- Make up record charts together with the family.
- Guide the parents through an example. Discuss a variety of incidents to cover a range of possibilities, and write these down.
- Ask the child and/or parent to fill out the chart relating to the last incident, or to an imagined situation (if the intervention involves something not yet tried).
- Give feedback on how the parents and child have been doing.
- Brainstorm with the family to come up with as many hindering or complicating factors as possible, and ways of coping with them. Reminders of these coping strategies need to be written on the back of the monitoring sheets.

❖ *Record Charts*

A few guidelines may be useful for parents to design charts for themselves or their child to use. We have included some example record charts in the Appendices for you to use in your assessment (for example, 24-hour Chart, Appendix III-1; Daytime Chart, Appendix III-3; Split-day Chart, Appendix III-8). If the parents have used these, they may have an idea of their own ways to record. The other record charts in the Appendices may be useful early on in the therapy if the parents are not ready to draw up their own. Even when they are becoming more autonomous, they will probably need some guidance to draw up charts that are not too complicated, with not too much to record at each point. The charts need to be worded positively — for example, "How many nights can I stay dry?" rather than "How many wet nights?"

Charts usually work best if the child keeps the record (see "My Record Chart, Appendix III-5), if this is age-appropriate, with encouragement from the parents. This also helps the child to take some of the responsibility for change, so it encourages motivation. It is important to personalize the record by having the child's name on it and matching it to their interests or favorite colors. The record needs to include positive behaviors that the child may use to overcome the problem behavior, for example, controlling temper by going for a walk or listening to music. Keeping the chart in a prominent place, so that the progress made is highly visible, also helps the child to stay well motivated.

The charts can continue in the 24-hour or ABC format, or can take the form of a reward or star chart for the child. If using rewards in this way, it is important to make sure that the parents understand what will help to maintain the child's progress. An information sheet on reward systems, which we often give to parents, is included in Appendix II-9.

When the child completes a reward chart or a progress chart, progress should be recorded in a way that is very easy to see. This can be illustrated by an increase, such as in the number of stars obtained, or by a climb up the page, such as towards the top of a mountain (see Hobday and Ollier, 1999).

The following ideas for the design of reward charts can help them to be accepted by the child and therefore make them more likely to be used.

- Any writing on the chart needs to be in language simple enough for the child to read and understand, with lettering of an appropriate size.
- Drawings can be incorporated, especially if the child enjoys artwork. Otherwise the form can be decorated with the child's favorite objects or interests (e.g., football team mascots).
- Ladders, hills, steps, castles or paths are all good images to chart a child's increasingly improved progress. For example, Peter can reach for the stars at the top of the staircase, each step representing a sub-goal (see "Stairs to the Stars," Appendix III-9).
- The child should have the pleasure of being the one to put on the sticker or color in the next bit of the record.
- If they are willing, parents and siblings can also have parallel monitoring sheets (see "Parent's Record Chart," Appendix III-6). For example, an older brother can record whether he remembered to praise

Peter for feeding the cats each morning and evening, or a parent can use ABC charts to note how they responded to Cathy's sulking behavior.

- The child may wish to use a secret code to record the frequency of positive behaviors, especially if the behaviors being overcome are embarrassing.

- A special pen, perhaps one that writes in "gold" ink, that is used only for recording can be fun and can also help the child to feel valued and encouraged.

- At the beginning of the program, rewards can be given for keeping the records before there is even any change in the target behavior. If this is going to happen, the parent will need to ensure that the child understands why a reward has been earned.

- The child's favorite subjects can be used to record progress. For example, the child may wish to use rabbit stickers, or color another planet in the galaxy that has been prepared as the reward chart.

- Once they have been earned, rewards should never be taken away, even if the child's behavior deteriorates.

❖ *Contact With the Therapist*

The therapist can be involved both over the telephone and in the clinic or home appointments. Telephone contact can be most helpful after the beginning of each stage of the baseline and the treatment phases. Although, in your session you will have tried to cover all possible eventualities, there are often unforeseen problems and these are best handled immediately so that the child and parents are not thrown into a state of ambivalence, and give up early on.

Once the parents and child have demonstrated their competency in recording their progress, contact can be limited to clinic sessions, with the phone being used only in case of emergency. If the family calls too frequently, then be aware of dependency issues and work harder to help them be more independent (see chapter 5). While how often you see the family will be partly influenced by your workload, it is best to try to determine the correct pace of sessions for the family after discussion with them. The simpler cases involving fairly standard programs, such as panic attacks, are better seen more frequently, perhaps once a week, so that the client progresses quickly and gains sooner from reduced anxiety. Cases involving chaotic families can also benefit from weekly sessions, at least for the first few sessions, in order to tease out all the issues and establish a regular, dependable therapeutic relationship. For most cases, an appointment every two weeks is sufficient during the therapy phase, and some families may prefer them to be more widely spaced. Remember that if they are too infrequent at this stage, it can reduce momentum in progress and allow new factors to hinder adherence to the program. As you enter the review and follow-up stages, less frequent appointments are most appropriate, giving the parents and child opportunity to problem-solve for themselves. The appointments may drop to monthly, then quarterly if all continues to go well.

❖ Follow-up

The length of follow-up you do with a family will depend on your resources and on the nature of the case. Some child problems, such as conduct disorders, tend to have good short-term outcomes, but decline over time. Although the likelihood of slipping back is reduced by a broader style of working which aims to empower the parents, these children may benefit from follow-up which maintains an active approach by the parents, with slow withdrawal as the parents become more expert and as the child develops.

5

Creating Autonomy

The major goal in any therapy is to produce change that will remain over time without the need for further professional intervention. When working with parents, the goal is to provide them with the skills, knowledge and ways of thinking so that they are able to tackle re-emerging or new problems independently, in a manner that promotes positive and appropriate behavior and relationships.

❖ Reassessing

When a program is implemented, behaviors, emotions and situations will change. Sometimes these changes are related directly or indirectly to the program itself and sometimes they are the result of unforeseen circumstances. To keep therapy running smoothly a program often needs to change over time to reflect the changing situation.

Reviewing the reward charts or monitoring sheets with the parents will help you to discover together what changes have occurred for the better or worse. If the target behavior has worsened a great deal, or if progress is especially slow, it will be time to look at reasons for this. It may be a flaw in the program you have worked out together, or it may be that you have been working on the wrong behavior because your original formulation has focused on the wrong aspect. This is why it is wise to use the information gleaned from the progress of the program so far to reassess the situation. It may be that from your reassessment the program changes dramatically. For example, you may not have been fully aware of the complexity of the situation, as illustrated by the following case example.

Case Example

Luke was a 10-year old who was referred for deteriorating behavior. During the normal assessment, Luke's mother spoke of how she and her husband were previously separated, but had reunited, albeit tentatively. During our first few sessions, as general behavior guidelines were introduced, Luke's behavior continued to deteriorate and went on to include the setting on fire of a relative's shed.

Further assessment, looking at reasons why Luke had not responded to the changes made, revealed that there was a background tension revolving around the parents' relationship. It turned out that Luke's behavior tended to be worse just after his parents had been arguing or when tension was highest. When it was suggested that Luke might be behaving badly in order to unite his parents (in anger), suddenly it all fell into place. The parents did not make a clear break, letting Luke know that his behavior would not be able to keep them together, but that they were happy with the new situation. Luke accepted the situation, became ashamed of his "out of character" behavior and returned to the true and delightful Luke.

If you have truly involved the parents as co-therapists from the start, they will by now be able to come up with their own analysis of the situation. We know we have reached this point when a parent says something along the lines of "Well, it hasn't worked but we think we know why. We have noticed that whenever we are all rushing around, then that is when he's most likely to have one of his outbursts and refuse to do as he's told. Do you think he's picking up on our anxieties about being late?" When parents reach this point it is easy to help them accept a more family-oriented approach so that the whole family works to effect change.

When a child is not changing, it often helps to have a brainstorming session with the parents (for example, "Encouraging Change," Appendix I-5) to identify what barriers may be preventing progress.

❖ *Barriers to Progress*

Below we have outlined some common barriers to progress and how to help parents to overcome them.

Family dynamics

During therapy, assessing the quality of the progress is important because as one part of the family functioning changes, so too do other parts. Often, when one problem area is improving, another area goes into decline. For example, parents may find that as one child begins to show progress in independent toileting (and receives lots of praise), another child starts to "act up" (to gain some attention too). Family roles change and myths are challenged. This upset to the family dynamics is a common occurrence (Burnham, 1988), and requires attention until a new balance within the family is established. By discussing the likelihood of such occurrences with the family at the beginning of therapy, the parents are more likely to recognize these changes and learn to frame them in a more positive light.

Marital discord

Parents need to come to understand that their behavior toward each other does significantly influence their child's mental health. When there is a factor like marital disharmony, it is likely that there will be little or no long-term progress in helping the child to overcome problem behaviors (e.g., Halford and Sanders, 1989). Some basic rules such as not arguing or yelling in front of the children, learning conflict resolution skills, supporting each other and practicing positive communication styles in front of the children will all help both parents and their children.

The parents may need some help in their own right, and it will certainly be beneficial for you to see them without the child there, so that you can together come to some understanding about the needs of the child. You may find it helpful to use the activity "Encouraging change" (Appendix I-5) with the parents. Be careful not to be seen to be blaming them, even if you are sure that the marital relationship is the main factor blocking therapy. Sanders and Dadds (1993) recommend shifting the emphasis gradually from child problems to a more "reciprocal conceptualization" by getting parents to discuss how the referred problems "place considerable stress on the rest of the family and, in particular, the marriage" (p. 192).

Parental expectations

Many parents may expect a smooth and gradual improvement. They do not consider the probability of any slip-backs. When parents are expecting pitfalls and imbalances along the way, and are given some examples, they then begin to think in these terms and are more likely to see change, in whatever direction, as a positive thing. So they learn to generate their own solutions.

In addition, parental expectations of their child's behavior may be too high. They may need a greater understanding of what is within the "normal" range for age-appropriate behavior. Aiming for this, and not perfection, will probably produce an earlier resolution to the problem. Also, their expectations of themselves as parents may be too high, causing them to feel that they are failing when in fact they have made good progress.

Failure to consider all solutions

The sorts of solutions that parents can draw on as problems emerge are numerous, and may include changes in:

- routines
- behavioral contingencies
- activities for children
- contact with the extended family
- social circles, church, clubs
- accessing external support systems, e.g., government agencies.

Sometimes parents expect that the "therapy" will help their child, without realizing the potential effects of other areas of the child's life. An activity such as "Encouraging Change" (Appendix I-5) may be useful here. In our example in that activity, the need emerged for the child to join a club.

Failure to use support systems

Parents may have to gain skills and confidence in making changes, and initially require support to do so. An extended social circle, involving family members and friends, is known to buffer against stress — perhaps by broadening a person's coping repertoire, by promoting a normal perspective on problems, and because social support leads to higher self-esteem (Sarason et al., 1987). Extended family members such as grandparents, who are well known to the child, can be very useful — they can reinforce the program with praise on a regular basis, and also help to keep parents on track as well.

The benefits of learning to access mainstream, community or voluntary resources and support systems (such as parenting support groups, mental health support groups) are also well documented (for example, Thoits, 1986). They tend to be free, and are often easier to access than professional services. Community supports are likely to carry little or no stigma, and are more likely to offer support that is not time limited. Generally, they make the family members feel involved with their own community, with the possibility of family members returning service to others, thus empowering the family further.

Failure to generalize

In order for the family members to take on the active role of handling problems on their own, they need to learn ways to view problems constructively, skills to put in place, and to gain the confidence to use these. Only then will they be able to generalize their problem-solving approaches to new difficulties.

Learning to recognize a problem and decipher what it means is the first step. Parents each come with their own skills and it is essential to draw these out (see "Combined Strengths and Skills," Appendix I-3), and build on them creatively until they have a broad enough range of ideas and "tricks" to play with in analyzing their situation. Some examples include:

- Teaching them the steps of problem-solving — defining the problem, generating numerous solutions, choosing one and assessing the consequences (see D'Zurilla and Nezu, 1982; Forgatch and Patterson, 1989; Spivack et al., 1976).
- Teaching new ways of looking at the problem — "What has worked in the past?'; "What has changed with this problem?"
- The family brainstorm, where all members of the family describe their experiences with the problem, and then seek common ground for change (see "Family Viewpoint," Appendix I-7).
- Thinking "What positive things have resulted from this change?"
- Listing the skills the family has for dealing with problems, and seeing which ones could be used (and in which way) to work towards a resolution (see "Skill Mix," Appendix I-10).

Changes are not maintained

Once problems are becoming resolved, it is important for families to recognize the need to maintain changes by not slipping back into old patterns. Useful ways of thinking include "What must change for the problem to reappear?" "What problems might we expect in the future?" "What have we as a family learned from this episode?" Each of these can be brainstormed as a family exercise.

Prevention of problems is also dependent on maintaining positive relationships within the family — keeping communication open and a joint willingness to deal with issues. Depending on the needs and desires of the family it may involve regular family chat times or family meetings where progress and future goals are discussed. Perhaps the family need to take turns in sharing power, e.g., who is in charge of the TV remote control, or choosing which fast-food meal the family will have over the weekend.

Some changes will not be maintained because a child has reached a different developmental stage. For example, if a goal for a 5-year-old includes holding Mom's hand when walking back from school, it will need to be changed to keeping with Mom, then as time goes on to staying within sight and waiting at the traffic lights.

The parents do not have confidence to go it alone

Instilling confidence is an important aspect of helping the family over the initial inertia of working independently. This needs to be done creatively and with enthusiasm — which will eventually transfer to your clients. Activities that can promote confidence include drawing out the skills they have demonstrated through their attempts to deal with problems, with their current household rules and routines, with their relationships, and with the knowledge they have demonstrated. After all, the changes we tend to suggest make up only a tiny part of the whole business of parenting, and they are more than likely doing 90 per cent of the job very well indeed. Getting parents (and children) to list their strengths early on keeps the focus on what they can do, as opposed to what they are having problems with. When there are two parents who are together, then a useful exercise could be to look at their individual strengths and put them together. From this they may wish to decide which other strengths they would like as a couple, and what they would like to work on (see "Combined Strengths and Skills," Appendix I-3).

❖ Family Practices

Another way to boost confidence and to maintain therapy gains over time is to promote those family practices that have been shown by research to have general benefits. Promoting parents' "attunement" to their child's development enhances their child's sense of competence, and increases parent support and appreciation for their child's problem-solving abilities (Shumow, 1998). With more competent parents, it can be useful to recommend specific texts on general child behavior management, such as *Taming Toddlers* (Green, 1999), *Love & Limits: Guidance Tools for Creative Parenting* (Crary, 1994), and *Raising Emotionally Intelligent Teenagers: Parenting with Love, Laughter, and Limits* (Elias et al., 2000).

Specific practices that are easy to build on current parenting skills include:

- Parents should be encouraged to make sure they are saying positive things to their children — this doesn't have to be in the manner of "I love you," but can be lots of little praises through the day for what the child does, or how nicely they ask for something.

- Increased sleep has been reported to solve a variety of childhood problems. The bedtime routine may need to be at an earlier time slot, with lots of rewards for going to bed. Use a video recorder, if available, to make sure that any missed favorite TV programs can be watched at another time.

- Exercise can raise the social status of children as well as having considerable health benefits (Gross et al., 1985). Sport can offer a new social scene and be appropriate for children with social problems as it can offer a structured setting. Encourage parents to choose something their child enjoys.

- Family activities do wonders for opening up communication between family members, and conversation in the context of shared activities promotes parents' awareness of their child's developmental level (Shumow, 1998). It is important that each child gets some individual attention each day, preferably from each parent. Having a weekly family meal, a game evening or an outing keeps people in touch (even teenagers can cope with one meal a week!).

- Limit the use of television. Children who watch for hours and who see programs meant for adults are more likely to have nightmares, fears and worries (Blechman, 1985). It is generally advisable to use the television not as a babysitter, but as a reward for quiet time, homework, reading and so on.

- If the television is off, the mealtime can create a perfect opportunity for the family to discuss what has happened in their day, to share new jokes, and to communicate with each other. It is also a perfect opportunity for parents to set an example on how to communicate. However, this is not recommended if parents are very critical of their children so that it becomes a very negative experience.

- Family time over weekends and evenings has been shown to reduce the influence of delinquent friends. Young people who spend a large amount of time with their parents are less likely to be involved in drugs, theft and burglary (Warr, 1993).

- Children like to know that parents are interested in them. Knowing where children are, maintaining rapport with them, and a "respectful" parent—child relationship, all help to maintain a positive relationship and to reduce the risk of adolescent substance abuse (e.g., Cohen and Rice, 1995). A practical way of implementing this is for parents to remember to ask their children about how their day has been — what did they do and how did they feel about things? If children feel that their parents love and care for them, then they are less likely to get into drugs or early sex, and they suffer less emotional distress (Klein, 1997).

- Weak or soft parenting does not help children who need guidance in their behavioral, emotional, spiritual and moral development. Strong, warm, consistent, positive parenting gives a child a sense of trust and security. Behavioral programs help put the parents back running the show — for example, the *Positive Parenting* program (Sanders et al., 1996 a,b,c,d), the *Parent, Adolescent and Child Training Series* (Herbert, 1996 a,b) and *Early Childhood Parenting Skills* (Abidin, 1996).

- Physical punishment is never appropriate. Rewards work much better in the long run and will not damage a child's self-esteem.

- Parents who work hard to show a united front are less likely to find that their children play one against the other.

- Parents need to be aware that marital discord is a predictor of child disorder, even when other risk and protective factors are considered (Dadds and Powell, 1991; Dadds, 1992). Thus, if marital problems do exist, they may need to be addressed either first, or concurrently (see "Barriers to progress," earlier in this chapter).

- Research suggests that under-involved parents (Iannotti et al., 1992), or those that argue a lot tend to have children who suffer from depression (Seligman, 1992). It is therefore important to encourage parents to be involved with their children and not to argue in front of them.

- Parents need to be sensitive to their child's particular needs. For example, children can suffer as a result of looking younger than they are, being overweight, having a sibling close in age, being young in their year at school, being socially isolated, and so on.

- Children benefit from having some responsibility in the house, such as a chore. It must be something they are able to achieve, and should be routinely rewarded to develop a sense of power in their world.

- Children need to be allowed to have some mess. One suggestion (Blechman, 1985) is for parents to choose an area that can be messy until a set time, e.g., Sunday. Have a "Sunday box" where everything goes last thing at night until Sunday, when they all get put away properly.

- Reading frequently with their children will help parents to instill a sense that learning is fun. Older children benefit most from reading aloud to their parents while younger ones usually prefer that parents read to them.

Sharing a good book can have both parent and child laughing together, while at the same time improving an important skill (Clarke-Stewart, 1998). If parents are very negative, however, they may have to learn how to make this a positive experience for their child.

- Playing with children is very important. Not only does it keep parents in touch with their child's abilities and interests but it has also been shown to help children both skill-wise and emotionally. Webster-Stratton (1992 b) reports that children learn not only to resolve conflicts and problem-solving, but that make-believe play with young children leads to improved vocabulary, value development, imagination and more positive self-esteem. Not only are the children less likely to have behavior problems, they are also more creative.

❖ *Closure*

It is important to work towards finishing with the parents as well as the child. It is good practice to recognize together when they are becoming able to resolve their own difficulties, and offer a limited number of further appointments. A further difficulty often arises at this point, which is the parents' and child's way of demonstrating how useful they have found the sessions to be. Do not despair, or be tempted to take over; rather, encourage them to tackle this in the way they have come to understand.

Rehearsal for slip-backs is a good item to include in the last few sessions. This will help the parents to feel confident that they can cope with whatever befalls. This can be done through role-play with all the family, or through discussion.

Many parents benefit from a final summary letter setting out the progress that has been made, and how they can use the skills they now have to meet future difficulties. This is an approach regularly used with cognitive analytic therapy (Ryle, 1990) and which is easily adapted to other approaches. In our example, it is the role of the parents in achieving the progress made that is emphasized.

Example Summary Letter

Dear John and Jenny,

As we have now come to the end of Fiona's sessions with me, I am writing to summarize the progress we have made.

First assessment –

Fiona was referred because of her stomach pains, which had been found to have no medical cause. The information you gave me, together with an assessment of Fiona at that first appointment, helped us to discover that she was very anxious in very many ways. Her stomach pains were a symptom of this.

You were able to pinpoint many areas of Fiona's life which caused her stress. These included the trauma of seeing her dog run over and her difficulties in settling after your two recent house moves. She was also very jealous of her sister, Cathy. In our third session Fiona told us how she was being bullied at school.

The approach we took and progress made –

Fiona benefited from some individual work on overcoming trauma and learning some anxiety management techniques. You were able to help her to learn new ways of coping with her anxiety at home, and making her feel valued. You spoke to the school and the teachers intervened so that Fiona is no longer bullied. You have helped her to gain in confidence and make new friends who have come over to play with her. She has recently been to stay overnight with a friend. You have helped her to overcome her fear of the dark.

You have started "family times" at home and have helped Cathy to become aware of her little sister's needs. The two girls are now much closer than they have ever been, but there are still some difficult times. Fiona appears to be less jealous of Cathy, as you have helped her to understand why Cathy has extra privileges. Your own idea of a timeline drawn up to help Fiona know when she will get the same privileges has proved very valuable.

As parents, you have demonstrated an increase in understanding the emotional and psychological needs of both your children. You have agreed that you will spend some time each week discussing their needs together, plan an approach to help either of them as necessary, and will back up each other as appropriate.

Fiona's present problem –

Fiona still has some areas of difficulty, such as being very anxious in recreational games, but you have worked out a plan with her teacher for tackling this. If the plan does not work, you will have a talk with the staff member concerned, and meanwhile seek to build up Fiona's confidence in other areas.

If the original problems reappear –

Your new ways of communicating with Fiona have reduced the likelihood of her becoming so anxious again. However, if she does, your plan is first to assess the situation, possibly by using the activity "Encouraging Change." You will then be able to form a plan to help her, remembering to adapt it to be age-appropriate.

I think it is highly unlikely that you will need any further appointments with me. However, if you would like a long-term review within the next six months, please contact my secretary. If it is longer than that, you will need a re-referral from your family doctor.

Best wishes for the future.

6 ❖

Parents With Different Needs or Circumstances

❖ Silent Parents

Most parents, if they have come to the session, are prepared to talk to you. However, you may find that with some, they do not understand the need to be included in therapy, thinking you can "fix our kid." They may tolerate being in the room but remain virtually silent. Other parents may feel shy or embarrassed in your presence, and be difficult to engage. Although the guidelines presented in chapter 1 will greatly assist you in helping these parents to talk to you, it can still be very discouraging.

As with any client, if they remain in the room then they are participating in the session. Do not give up on them or tell them off for not taking an active role. We have found the best way is to talk gently in a one-sided presentation of how you see the problem, presenting alternatives, for example "Maybe Susie is very anxious at this time, or maybe she is feeling very angry about something." Check it out with them as you proceed. Even the quietest parents will usually nod or grunt in agreement or disapproval. You may think it appropriate to inform them from current research — "I have asked you to work with me to help Susie overcome her difficulties because we know from research that parents being involved can greatly influence the success of working with the young person." Even if you can quote references and statistical probabilities, do so only if you are sure the parents will appreciate it.

Tell the parents clearly how some parents are worried that they will be blamed for their child's behavior, but you realize there are many reasons why a child has problems. Stress that the fact that they have brought their child here for therapy indicates that they are caring parents who want help for their child. This is also a good time to begin to show you have some understanding of what their child may be going through. For example, "Many of the children I see with stealing problems have recently gone through a difficult time, sometimes at home, or it may be at school or with their friends. Now, it may be that Jo has had a hard time and maybe we don't know what it is. But if you have noticed that she is breaking away from you, taking less care of herself, not responding to requests like she used to, then something may be going on. We need to work together to try to find out what it is."

After this very gentle approach, parents usually begin to appreciate the need to cooperate, and even the most shy will begin to contribute if the information given by them is met with approval and thanks for its usefulness. Sometimes, quiet parents enjoy using pen and paper tasks rather than sitting around discussing their child's welfare, so it may be helpful to use some of the activities mentioned in chapters 4 and 5.

❖ Dependent Parents

Some parents will see you as the person who will sort out all their family problems and therefore they become totally dependent on you. Alternatively, they may become so used to coming to sessions (seeing them as family outings where everyone has fun) that they are reluctant to give them up.

Dependency decreases as autonomy increases. Read through chapter 5, on autonomy, again to check you are following all the guidelines suggested there.

Do talk to parents about how taking responsibility for handling family problems can be scary, and that you will not leave them floundering, but continue to support them as necessary. If parents do phone "in crisis," assess just how critical the situation is and, if the problem does not justify an early appointment, offer them an appointment that will give them time to be able to sort things out for themselves, but not leave them feeling abandoned.

A useful exercise to show this family what is happening is outlined in "The Absent Therapist" (Appendix I-1).

❖ *Aggressive Parents*

If you are expecting a parent who may be aggressive, then make sure you have the exit to your room clear for both him or her and yourself so that you can escape if you feel unsafe, and your clients can storm out rather than hit you! These are the parents you must never see late in the day or over your lunch break when there is no one else around.

When parents are behaving aggressively, the first thing to think about is whether everyone is safe. Consider any children around first, and if the parents have weapons or appear to be threatening anyone's life, call Security. If you have a personal alarm, then use it.

If there is no immediate physical threat, different strategies may be appropriate. If they become aggressive in front of the children, see if you can take the children from the room saying, for example "I can see you have some difficult matters which need to be discussed, so perhaps Charlie could play in the waiting area while we speak."

If the aggression is verbal, rather than physical, you may be able to calm the parent down. Speak in a slow, calm manner without being confrontational and agree with the parent whenever possible. Do not argue with them, but apologize if what you have said has upset them. Reiterate that you are all here to help their child, using the child's name. Be careful not to try to pull in the sympathy of the other parent but address them both. Invite them to sit down to discuss the matter quietly with you and say you acknowledge their anger. You may wish to say something like "Of course you feel angry that the waiting list is six months long — I myself am angry that people have to wait so long." While they are angry, it is a bad time to reason with them, but it may be possible later on to explain what you have or haven't done, and why. Even if wrongly blamed, strong denials of your supposed actions will only make the aggressive parent angrier.

If you cannot calm the parent down, don't be a hero — call for some help.

❖ *Parents Who Have Abused Their Children*

Working with these parents can be particularly difficult. Therapists will need to be exceptionally careful to keep their own feelings in check if they find that a child they have been working with has, in fact, been abused. Jones et al. (1987) outline typical feelings that may arise in the therapist. These include denial, anger, guilt, fear, horror and despair. If other professionals have to intervene following disclosure, then they may also feel jealousy, resentment and/or omnipotence.

It is important to keep very calm with these families and not to confront them. Confronting them may lead to their withdrawal from therapy and possibly put the child at greater risk. While you can remain objective, recognizing the parents' own needs and feelings of failure, or even remorse, you will be able to work alongside them. Your work with these parents will probably be quite focused on their needs. Mash and Johnston (1990) found that parental characteristics and environmental circumstances contributed most to the parent-child stress that led to abuse. The child's behavior was of less impact. Other research has found that parents who have abused their children often grew up in abusive homes themselves (Barker, 1995), tend to have an authoritarian parenting style, and have little awareness of their child's level of ability, interests, or needs (Wolfe, 1987). Therefore, expect to take much longer to reach the stage where the parents can work with you as co-therapist. Although you will be working toward this goal, it may not be attainable.

You will usually be in the position (whether you like it or not) of watching the situation to ensure that the child is safe. It may well be that the decision to let the family "go it alone" is made only after a multidisciplinary meeting, when the other professionals concerned are convinced that the parents have benefited from the therapy offered. Following this, there may be further input and support from social services when you have completed your work with the parents.

❖ Uncooperative Parents

There are many reasons why parents can be uncooperative. We shall look at three that are commonly encountered. First, parents may have strong reasons for maintaining the status quo, and this may not have become apparent at the initial assessment. The most usual reason is that focusing on the child's difficulties avoids addressing their own. An example is a child who is presenting with sleep difficulties. It may be that the toddler has been permitted to sleep in the parents' bed to provide an excuse for the parents to avoid intimacy. An approach focusing on the child's difficulty will fail to address the problem. Couple therapy would be more appropriate.

The lack of cooperation may be masking another difficulty. For example, uncooperative parents may be quietly aggressive parents, they may be silent because they are shy parents, or they may have mental health difficulties of their own. The guidelines under each of these headings will help them to move forward with their child.

A further reason could be that they have never formed an attachment with their child, and see no reason to help with the therapy now. Look back at your original assessment of the family to see if this likely and consider whether the parents have been positive or negative about their child to date. For a fuller description of how to measure attachment, see Hughes (1999).

❖ Parents Who Are Never Satisfied

Whenever you find that just as you help the family to overcome one problem, another reappears, this may well be a dependent parent in disguise.

The level of dependency becomes worrying if the parents continue to present their child with psychological problems which, when assessed, do not exist. It may be that the parents need to learn about child development and to give them a more complete idea of what is "normal" for a child of that age is sufficient to help them. Supplement this with suggestions of a book to buy (for example, Green, 1984; Webster-Stratton, 1992a; Montgomery and Morris, 1988) or information sheets for different age groups.

If parents continue to seek help — perhaps going from one therapist to another — it may be that they are an example of Munchausen's Syndrome by proxy or factitious disorder by proxy (*DSM IV;* American Psychiatric Association, 1994). If you suspect this, it is important to communicate with all the other professionals involved and then work together to help the family. Usually involving mothers, these parents tend to have poor partner support and demonstrate unsure, inconsistent parenting skills, with poor coping abilities (Marcus et al., 1995). This disorder is reported to lead to a high level of stress among the professionals involved (Goldfarb, 1998), and calls for a multidisciplinary approach, with adequate staff support. (For a recent book on the topic, see Parnell and Day, 1998).

❖ *Parents With Mental Health Problems*

If a parent appears ambivalent, unmotivated, or is dealing with grief or loss, they may well be suffering from depression. If you are not yourself qualified to assess the parent for depression, you will need to refer on. If this is clinical depression, then the parent will be unlikely to be able to help his or her child until their mood has lifted. The effect that maternal depressive mood has on perceptions of the child's difficulty is documented by Forehand et al. (1986). They stress the importance of the maternal perceptions, and how these should be considered as part of the initial assessment of the referred behavior problem.

Other disorders may also present a barrier to therapy, such as obsessive compulsive disorder. This will be especially true if the parent's problems are a more serious case of the child's difficulties.

If a parent has generalized anxiety, and the child is presenting with anxiety, then it is possible to work with the parent at the same time as with the child. While you would be wise to encourage the parent to seek help in their own right, it is possible for both parent and child to benefit as you begin to educate them, for example in the symptoms of anxiety. Sometimes parents who have been, or are, in the same situation as the child are extremely effective in helping their child to change because of their increased understanding of how it feels to be anxious.

❖ Split Families

Separated parents will need to become aware of some of the feelings that their children may have. The division of loyalties is often very difficult for the child to manage. This raises issues about who should be at the session. Be careful not to become part of the parents' dispute by being seen to take sides. Confident therapists sometimes find it useful to have a session with both parents (without the child present) to discuss ways to minimize the difficulties for the child. Obviously, this will depend on a number of factors including their new partner's views of this arrangement, and the parents' levels of hostility toward each other. Your aims should be the same as in any other therapy — to encourage the parents to be able to move towards working "in parallel" to promote the best outcome for the child.

There are a number of factors that will help the parents to achieve the arm's length friendliness with each other which will be most beneficial to the child. These are outlined in our information sheets for parents of children in split families (Appendices II-2 and II-3). For other information that may be useful for these parents, see the marital discord section in chapter 5 under "Barriers to Progress," and "Aggressive Parents" earlier in this chapter. Freeman et al. (1998) review guidelines regarding the measures that parents can take to help their children.

Foster "Caregivers" or "Parents" and Adoptive Parents

❖ ▬▬▬▬▬▬▬▬▬▬▬▬▬▬▬▬▬▬▬▬▬▬▬▬

Parents who have children with a previous history of moving between families do not know the full extent of the effect of the child's past experiences. A significant number of fostered and adopted children have been abused or neglected, and this brings with it a range of emotional disturbances that often lead to behavior problems (Hobday and Lee, 1995). Gaining trust is a common problem, and many children will spend a lot of time "testing" how new parents respond to provocation. Although this may only be an attempt to re-create familiar patterns of discipline, it can cause the parents to feel inadequate. As adolescence approaches, the young person's identity becomes very important and they may want to spend renewed energy delving into their past and trying to make sense of it all. This can bring up issues for the parents, posing questions over their right to be the young person's parents.

Many complex psychological processes are present in the relationship between the adoptive or foster child and the parents. Some of these are reflected in the relationship with the therapist. For example, the foster caregivers usually see themselves in a semi- or completely professional role, working with their child. This can make working with them much easier when using the approach we have outlined in this book because they already see themselves as therapists. It is important to make sure they understand that they are providing parenting as well.

With adoptive parents the task is more complex. They may still be working on becoming a parent to the child. In this situation it is more important to establish them as parents before working with them to help them gain enough skills to help the child overcome psychological difficulties. The material on promoting positive attachment, in Fahlberg (1994), is very useful here.

Parents of Children With Chronic Health Conditions

One common problem with children suffering from chronic conditions is that their medical state can sometimes appear bigger than the child. It is important to work with the parents to focus on helping the child, rather than focusing on their disorder. Secondary gains regarding the condition need to be assessed to see if they are impeding progress in development, e.g., is the child managing to remain dependent on parents when he/she should be demonstrating more independence? Equally, parents can compensate by doing too much for the child, or letting them "get away with" a lot more than their peers. Because of hospital admissions or ongoing medication, families often have a distorted lifestyle, perhaps unavoidably. It can be useful to look at how the child and family can normalize their lifestyle as much as possible.

Very often, these parents are grieving for their happy healthy child, and have not come to terms with their child's condition. Time is usefully spent discussing with them their feelings about the illness and helping them to find appropriate literature, or to approach the relevant medical staff for further information. Cadranel (1991) further discusses counseling of parents with children with chronic health conditions.

Parents Under Constant Stress

Where there are external factors causing stress in a family, parents sometimes seek help for their children who are showing signs of distress. The potential influence of constant stress on children is mediated by "the quality and sensitivity of the parents' interactions with their children" (Webster-Stratton, 1990, p. 303).

Very often, these parents are in a state of "learned helplessness," being unable to do anything about the situation in which they find themselves. Obviously, if the stressor is a major life event like divorce or the illness or death of a close family member, therapy will focus on helping the parents to come to terms with their situation and do the best they can for their child.

In some cases, the parents may also need to use a problem-solving approach to begin to find some way to change their circumstances. This is illustrated in the case example below.

Case Example

Steven, 9, was the only son of Mr. and Mrs. Roberts. He was referred by a pediatrician for therapy regarding psychosomatic stomach pains. On initial interview the parents were obviously agitated and upset, and began to blame their neighbors. Apparently, there had been an ongoing dispute with the neighbors, which had resulted in Mrs. Roberts being hit in front of her son, and Steven being bullied in school by the children of the neighbor's family.

Anxiety management sessions were arranged with Steven, with Mr. and Mrs. Roberts taking part in the sessions. Although they all left the sessions feeling relaxed and at ease, they were unable to practice any skills at home, as they were immediately under siege with graffiti on their walls and abuse hurled at them from the neighbor. Meeting with the parents alone provided the opportunity to begin to clarify the situation and look at the way ahead. After a "pros and cons" exercise, looking at reasons to do something about the situation and reasons to ride it through, they were able to take the step of talking to a lawyer. The subsequent court injunction freed them to decide that they would like to move anyway, so they took steps to arrange a housing transfer.

Once they felt empowered to begin to change the situation, they were able to address their son's needs. Steven responded well as his parents' confidence grew.

Conclusion

Within this book we have outlined ways of working with parents which may be new to many therapists. It may be that the ideas are too far from your own practice for you to be able to accept them. However, we hope that you have been able to glean a few ideas for use in your approach to parents. We have not purported to have all the answers, but we have used our collective experience, and the experience of our colleagues and clinical psychologists in training, to try to make sense of our practice and approach. This is the first attempt to document it in this form.

Our message may be stronger and more in favor of the parent as therapist than are other texts. However, we feel justified in taking this stance through findings reported from the work of others who have researched the factors that lead to successful therapy. But it must be borne in mind that parents have a parental role to fulfill before they can learn the basics of becoming the parent therapist.

The activities we have introduced have arisen from situations within our work where we have needed to put across ideas in a clear and concise manner. Each of the activities and suggestions has been evaluated within our own clinical practice, albeit with relatively small numbers. Further study of these is welcomed.

Our first creative therapy title, *Creative Therapy: Activities with Children and Adolescents* (Hobday and Ollier, 1999), which features activities for working with children, has been welcomed as a very practical resource, especially for new therapists. It is our hope that this present text will prove to be just as useful, venturing as it does into more of a teaching arena. At the very least, we hope you can take from it some feeling that you are not working alone, but others have difficulties with certain parents, and have tackled them in the ways we have suggested.

Working with parents is not always easy, but it can be an enjoyable experience that can prove rewarding. Empowering the parents, rather than taking away from the therapist, can help you to feel empowered to tackle the next challenge. Throwing around ideas with parents, who are themselves becoming more and more skilled, is very good for helping you to become more creative in your own approach to therapy.

But what about your colleagues? Here is a valuable resource for your own development as a therapist. Never forget the importance of supervision and case discussions for generating new ideas and increasing your own creative approach. This book is a spin-off from just such working relationships, whereby we as psychologists were able to use each other's ideas to generate solutions to difficult situations. In these days of multidisciplinary teams it may be very difficult to have contact with another therapist who has similar training to yourself. However, anyone who works therapeutically with children and parents will be able to understand the situations you find difficult, and if you brainstorm approaches that may work, you will greatly enrich your therapeutic approach.

Appendices

Appendix I

❖ *Appendix I-1*

The Absent Therapist

Aim

To help families to resolve difficulties without the help of the therapist. This exercise is useful at the end of the therapeutic intervention, especially with families who are having difficulty becoming independent.

Materials

Paper, pen, extra chair.

Method

The activity is spread over several weeks and takes the following course:

1. Invite the family to their next appointment but explain that you will not be there. Suggest that they imagine you are in your usual chair and work out together what you would say when they discuss their problems. Encourage them to take notes and leave them for you. Keep well out of the way during the session, so that the family arrives, uses the room and leaves without seeing you.

2. After you have read through the notes, feed back over the telephone how well they've done and suggest that this is the way forward for them.

3. The next session with the empty chair can be at home or, if they would still like an outing, at the beach, at a picnic, or over a meal in a restaurant. Again, ask the family to keep notes.

4. Maintain enough contact to be able to suggest when the "chair" is not really needed any more. Stress the importance of keeping up the meetings on a regular basis. Rename them "family meetings."

5. Encourage the family still to keep notes, but of their own thoughts and decisions made during the family meeting.

6. Withdraw completely once the family meetings are up and running on a regular basis.

During this process, it is important not to be drawn back into seeing the family when crises arise. Instead, encourage them to hold an extra meeting of their own and use their own skills to address any crisis.

The exercise will not be successful if you criticize their ways of handling situations. Do this only if their approach is likely to cause major problems or if anyone is at risk. If it is only a matter of style — for example, they think you would agree to 8:30 bedtimes for all the children — then praise them that they as a family have made the decision, and remind them that all decisions can be reviewed if they find they do not work for their family.

N.B. Some families may not be willing to attend if the therapist will not be there. In this case, when they arrive, explain you will leave for a while and set out an agenda for them to discuss their difficulties and how to resolve them. As before, ask them to make notes. Leave them to perform the exercise, but reappear near the end of the session to read through the notes. Give them encouraging feedback, then follow this activity from step 3 above.

Appendix I-2

Balanced Messages

Aim
To illustrate the ease with which we can confuse others if we do not communicate clearly.

Materials
A thimble or other small object.

Method
This game is a variation of the "hot and cold" game, also known as "hunt the thimble." Initially, get the youngest or most vulnerable family member to be the first to be "in." Play a straight game where he or she has to leave the room while everyone else decides where to hide the thimble. Ask the "in" person to come back in and stand in the middle of the room, and the others then use the words "hotter," "colder," "warmer," etc., to guide the "in" person to the thimble. Feedback about being "hot" or "cold" needs to be given each time the "in" person has taken one or two steps or has changed direction.

With the next "in" person (it is best to choose the least vulnerable person, perhaps a parent) do the same but, while hiding the thimble, explain to the remaining family members that they are not to use "hot" or "warm," but rather can feed back to the "in" person only when they are "cold" or "colder." When the "in" person returns and starts the game, they are likely to become quickly frustrated. Do not let them go too long before asking them if they want to give up. Explain what has happened, and ask the "in" person to describe how they felt. Use this to illustrate how children need positive guidance, not just telling off, in order to help them stay on the right track. Repeat this with the same person, giving only "warm" and "hot" and compare how much faster that same person is able to find the thimble; that is, they can work out what to do. Again, ask the "in" person how different it felt to get positive rather than negative feedback.

Variation I: Tell Me Sooner
Give the "in" person all feedback, but make family members delay it by three seconds, to illustrate how praise and feedback work best (are not confusing) when they are given immediately.

Variation II: Tell Me Faster

Give the "in" person feedback, but only every second time they have got warmer or colder (to illustrate the importance of consistency). This one is a bit tricky, so it is best used with families who have a good grasp of the concept of the game.

Appendix I-3

Combined Strengths and Skills

Aim

To illustrate strengths and skills which parents have, that can be used in parenting. To emphasize the importance of parents working together.

Materials

Paper, pens, paste or stapler. For variation, also index cards and a box or envelope.

Method

Take a sheet of paper and write as a heading "Combined Strengths and Skills." Cut it vertically in half, in a zigzag fashion. One half is then given to each partner, who proceeds to write a list of his or her own strengths and skills, as close to the zigzag cut as possible. Give the parents some ideas about the sorts of skills and strengths they may want to include — e.g., personal characteristics, skills they can pass on to their children, supportiveness towards each other, brain power. If they find this task difficult to do, you may need to help them to get started by using your knowledge of them to make some suggestions.

When each partner has completed their list join the pieces of paper together again — perhaps pasting or stapling them on to another sheet. Promote discussion between the parents about how they can pool their skills practically to help the child overcome his or her difficulties. See example, page 50.

Variation: Whose Strengths and Skills?

For families that are particularly stuck you may wish to give them a number of strengths — each written on a card — to pull out of a box or envelope. As they pull each one out, they can decide which parent is best at this thing, discarding those which are not appropriate. Follow this with the rest of the activity as outlined above.

Appendix I-4

Creating Cooperation

Aim

To provide an opportunity for family members to work together towards a common goal, in an atmosphere that promotes cooperation, cohesion and humor and which illustrates the positive gains of working together.

Materials

A small, old magazine which has had all the page numbers removed, and the pages separated. The material in the magazine should be equally relevant to young and old.

Method

Explain the task to the family, and tell them that you will time them. (The timing is not important as such, but helps to get the family members working quickly together.) Ask them to sit around a table, or on the floor in a circle, and put the mixed up pages in the middle for the family members to sort out into the correct order. Start them off, setting the timer. Leave them to it, noting which sort of role each family member tends to take on — who is a leader, who goes with the flow, who makes sure everyone has a job. Afterwards, help the family to realize the importance of every family member's role.

Note

This is most appropriate for families with children over 12 years of age, where all members are literate. Alternatively, you can use a calendar, or a children's book with which younger children will be familiar. Create your own version to suit the family.

Variation: Whose Turn to Be Boss?

This game can be used in the same way, but with several magazines. Each time a magazine is sorted, a different family member is in charge. Time as before, and help the family to discuss different strategies used by different family members. Lead on to discuss the different "strengths" of each member of the family (be sure that each family member has at least one strength, e.g., enthusiasm). The game can be organized to make everyone boss for one round. The resulting chaos can reinforce the need for everyone to be different.

Appendix I-5

Encouraging Change

Aim

To help parents to become aware of factors that are preventing change.

Materials

Large sheet of paper, thick marker, goal sheet (Appendix III-4).

Method

Take a large piece of paper and write on it "What must change for _____ to change?" This gives you the opportunity to help them to think of many different aspects of their child's well-being, involving all the other people in the child's life, as in the example. Write down everyone's suggestions, making sure you cover all areas of difficulty. Circle all those that can be influenced by the parents or therapist and work on these.

Work out what barriers there are to the child making changes. Find a goal, which includes help by the adults, for each of the items that need to be changed. Use the goal sheet to record these. From this, pick out two or three goals to work on immediately.

Example

Barriers and Goals from "What Must Change"

1. Area: <u>Friendships</u>
   Barrier: Bill is too shy to invite anyone to play after school
   Goal: Mom to talk to Mark's mother and see if Mark would like to come to play.

2. Area: <u>Joining a club</u>
   Barrier: He'd like to go to karate, but there's no bus into town on Saturday morning.
   Goal: Dad will ask Stephen's mom if she could take him if we helped pay for the gas.

3. Area: <u>Schoolwork</u>
   Barrier: Bill's too shy to tell his teacher he needs help.
   Goals: a) For now, we can tell the teacher about his problem so that she knows he's struggling.
           b) He needs to learn how to ask for help so he could join the social skills group when it's next offered.

4. Area: <u>Feeling valued</u>
   Barrier: If we tell him he's important he doesn't believe us, so we've given up bothering.
   Goal: To start spending special time with him, looking at the things he's good at, and to try telling him he's important again; to follow the guidelines in the information sheet.

5. Area: <u>Calming down</u>
   Barrier: Don't know — perhaps all the other things that bother him.
   Goal: To sort out some of the other things, then teach him how to be less anxious.

6. Area: <u>We get irritated</u>
   Barrier: Habit !!
   Goal: a) To watch each other and take turns dealing with him when he's being difficult. To take over as one or the other starts to get upset.
           b) To keep looking for positive things about him.

7. Area: <u>Time with Dad</u>
   Barrier: Dad doesn't have much time with a seven-day-a-week job.
   Goal: For Bill to go to work with Dad at the garden center once a month and help him with the planing.

In the example given, it is easy to see how the parents have recognized their own responsibility for sorting out some of Bill's problems. Initially they had shown a reluctance to change the family routine to address Bill's problems, but this exercise proved to them that everything could not be left to the therapist.

Make sure the parents take a copy of the list of Barriers and Goals, so that this establishes their role as the main people who will facilitate change. It is also important that you follow through your goals promptly (e.g., put Bill's name down for the social skills group and find out the dates) as this will help you to maintain a good therapeutic relationship with the family.

Family Needs

Aim

To help each family member to see that problems arise through people's needs, and that each of them can work towards meeting their own and other members' needs.

Materials

Paper, colored markers.

Method

This activity is best used with children over 12 and adults. Talk to the parents about the way that incidents can be looked at in terms of ABCs (see Appendix III-2) and then solutions can be found that reflect the needs of the people involved. Encourage the parents to write the problem in ABC format across the middle of the sheet of paper, e.g.,

Antecedent (Before)	Behavior (During)	Consequence (After)
Simon started playing with Tom's Lego™	Tom hit Simon	I yelled at Tom

With each part of the problem behavior, family members can generate possible reasons why the A, B or C occurred, based on people's needs. Do not forget to include needs that apply to more than one member of the family, for example Tom and Simon need opportunities to learn to play with each other.

The needs that have been drawn out by the mother, from our example above, are as follows:

Simon has a need to play and a need to learn how to play with others.
Simon needs to learn what he can play with in Tom's room.
Simon needs to feel he's doing things with Tom.

Tom needs to keep control over his toys.
Tom needs to learn to tell me when Simon comes in.
Tom needs a special place to put toys that Simon can't get to.
Tom needs to come up with one or two things that he and Simon can play with together.

I need to establish some rules.
I need to learn to support Tom in letting him have special toys.

I need to have special time with Simon when Tom wants to play with his Lego™.
I need to learn to count to 10 when things get out of hand!

Tom and Simon need plenty of chances to learn how to play together, with some sort of help from me.

When this task is completed, then explore how each person can help to meet the needs of the family members.

Family Viewpoint

Aim

To help family members see that although the problem affects them all personally, each family member can work towards positive change.

Materials

Large sheet of paper, two different colored markers.

Method

This activity is best used with children over 6 and adults.

Write (or ask the parents to write) the nature of the problem in the middle of the page. Guide them to try to include causes, if known, and avoid blaming the child. For example, "Sam gets panicky and then he's very upset and angry" is better than "Sam goes berserk and upsets everyone. He's like a maniac. We can't take him anywhere."

Help each member of the family, including the child who has the problem, to write down the effects the problem has. For example, an 8-year-old (Mark) might write "I don't like him playing with my toys in case he throws them." The 6-year old with the problem (Sam) might ask you to write "I get scared, then everyone gets me angry." Mom might write "I get fed up with trying to control him — I feel it's all left to me to sort it out." Dad's contribution might be "I get angry because he's really lost it by the time I'm called to help."

Now have the family use the other color to write down what they can change. At this point they can write under other people's effects as well as their own, putting their name or initial by it. Some examples from the effects above would be:

I don't like him playing with my toys
I'll help you to find some that won't break for now — Mom
I could let him play with some of them, or I could play with him with his toys — Mark

I get scared, then everyone makes me angry
Try telling me you feel scared before you throw a tantrum — Mom
Come and talk to me, son — Dad

I get fed up with trying to control him
If you tell me when he first starts, I'll help — Dad
I could ask Dad to deal with it from the beginning — Mom

I get angry because he's awful by the time I see him
If I can help calm him down earlier I won't be so angry myself —
Dad
When you are angry I'll remind you to go and count to ten —
Mom

Help the family to put some of these ideas into practice —
perhaps adding some further suggestions for calming down — or
involving the other children more fully. In our example, Mark
could have been encouraged to play with Sam by Mom, saying
she would keep an eye on them until they could see that Sam was
more settled.

See also:
"Encouraging Change" (Appendix I-5).

Appendix I-8

Many Ways to Praise

Aim

To promote an emphasis on positive parenting, and to increase skills at using verbal rewards. This is a slight variation on "51 Ways to Praise" (Hobday and Ollier, 1999) and can be especially useful when a family is trapped in a cycle of negative interaction by illustrating that there are many ways of praising (it doesn't have to be repetitive), and many ways of making praise personal and enthusiastic. It is often helpful to do this exercise before introducing the activity "What Behaviors Can We Praise?" (Appendix I-11).

Materials

Colored markers, one large or several smaller sheets of paper, and paste or tape.

Method

Ask each parent, or each member of the family (if doing it as a family exercise), to come up with as many ways of saying "well done!" as possible. Ask the parents to write these down, either on one large sheet, or on many small sheets of paper stuck together. Ask each member of the family to pick out their favorite phrases by circling them in different colors. Be enthusiastic, encouraging the family to think of times when they may use these phrases. The "Many Ways to Praise" can be taken home and pinned up in a prominent place to act as a reminder to all the family.

Different families can aim for certain numbers of ways to praise. We often use 51, which may seem like a lot, but for this reason it can be a good number, providing the family members reach the goal and pleasantly surprise themselves. If families are stuck, try prompting them with the letters of the alphabet, e.g., A could be "Absolutely fantastic," B could be "Brilliant," and C could be "Cool." Some families may be motivated to head for 100. If the family members are not skilled verbally, the number may need to be reduced at the outset so that they are not disappointed — as few as 10 can work. The list can then be added to at the beginning or end of subsequent sessions.

This exercise can work well with all the family if children are old enough (teenagers) to take some responsibility for providing positive feedback to caregivers.

For families who are having difficulty adopting positive verbal rewards, the "Many Ways to Praise" list they generate can act as a cue where parents are asked to record which praise they use, when, and how often, with a goal of increasing the number of praises given over time.

Appendix I-9

Requests

Aim

To encourage positive communication by helping parents to discover different ways of making requests to their children. To help them determine which ways gain a positive response from their child, and why.

Materials

"Requests" record chart (Appendix III-7), a large sheet of paper, markers.

Method

Discuss with the parents the need to communicate clearly with their child. On the large piece of paper, brainstorm ways and means by which requests are commonly made — for example, indirectly, shouting, clearly, in long sentences, in competition with their favorite television programs.

Suggest that they complete the record chart (Appendix III-7) over the coming week.

When they return, having completed the task, discuss all the positive ways with them. If any negative ways have had an effect, discuss why this might be (fear, habit, they know she really means it now) and discuss whether this fits a positive parenting model.

Variation: All Our Requests

With adolescents it can be useful to do this as a family activity where the teenagers look at their requests to parents, as well as the parents looking at their requests to their children.

Appendix I-10

Skill Mix

Aim

To help parents to realize that they have skills and abilities that will help their child, and to introduce new skills they are acquiring.

Materials

Paper, pen.

Guidelines for Use

This activity is best used after some progress has been made in therapy, to consolidate the skills they brought to therapy and those they have learned. It is best used with parents who will not be offended by the suggestion that more skills will further assist them in helping their child.

Method

Draw an outline of a large mixing bowl in the bottom third of the page. Ask parents about skills or attributes that they each have that will help their child. Fill the mixing bowl with all the parents' established skills and abilities — if they give vague answers, see if you can help them pinpoint particular skills. Talk about all the skills and abilities that may still be needed and, if the parents do not feel they have them (or are still working on them), complete your illustration by having them "pour in" to the established skills mixture (see Figure 6). Try to have more "established skills" than "skills needed" so that the parents feel they are already quite well equipped to help their child.

Before leaving the task, emphasize what a powerful mix they already have and how the main ingredients are already there. The rest can be added as they learn new ways to help their child.

From this, get parents to think about how they can translate their skills into practical ideas on how to help their child. This may lead to a discussion about when one parent can take over because they have better skills. For example, one may be better than the other at sorting out quarrels. Some parents may want to learn from each other, but be very careful with this one in case they become resentful of each other's skills.

Figure 6   Sample Skill Mix

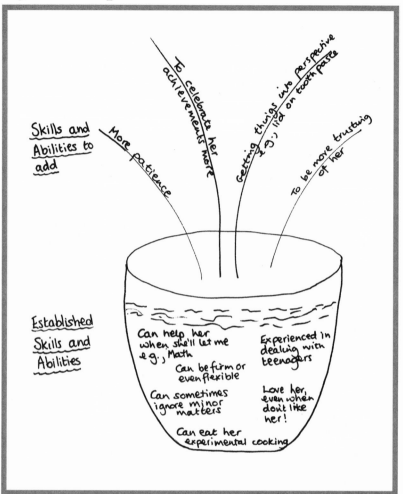

Appendix I-11

What Behaviors Can We Praise?

Aim

To help parents to become aware of the many positive behaviors that their children display.

Materials

Record chart (Appendix III-10) or paper. Some means of attaching the list to a prominent place, e.g., refrigerator magnets. Markers.

Method

Discuss with the parents the many activities that go on in a day. Talk about those that often go unnoticed, especially with a noisy, disruptive child. Invite them to make a list of praiseworthy behaviors in the session, which can be added to at home throughout the week. Suggest they put a tick by each one where they have remembered to praise, perhaps also recording where they have not praised. If the parent is likely to feel guilty about not praising, ask them to complete only the first two columns. When reviewing this exercise, see:

a) Who took part?

b) Who praises?

c) What has the family learned from this exercise? (Have they noticed any changes in themselves or their child?)

d) What kind of behaviors do they now consider praiseworthy?

e) Were there any other discoveries made by the family?

Appendix II

❖ Information Sheets

Appendix II-1

Aggressive Behavior in Teenagers

15 Ways to Deal With Your Teenager's Aggression

1. Do not be aggressive yourself — young people often imitate or model themselves on others' behavior.

2. When your son or daughter begins to become angry defuse the situation as far as possible by:

    a) not becoming angry yourself

    b) not picking up on angry words and responding to them

    c) walking away saying you'll discuss this issue later "when we are both calm"

3. If your teenager says "You hate me" because you have asked him or her to do something, you will need to sort out the issues. For example, say "No, I love you but I still want you to clean your room."

4. If your child is already angry, do not go into long explanations about "why." A better time to discuss reasons is later when you are both calm, "over a cup of tea."

5. When it is all over and things are calm, discuss the aggressive behavior. Work out what happened and how you both could have made things calmer.

6. Generally speaking, do not give in to the aggression. However, you may need to think about people's safety at the time.

7. Make sure your demands and expectations are realistic for a young person of that age.

8. Remember that some conflict is likely as your son or daughter moves from being a child to becoming an adult. This involves leading an increasingly separate life from you. Give your children appropriate privileges (like being allowed out late) and responsibilities (like feeding the dog) to show you have noticed they are growing up.

9. Focus only on the big issues — be prepared to overlook minor differences of opinion or minor wrongdoings so that there is less conflict with your teenager.

10. Encourage your teenager to talk things through rather than be aggressive. Thank her when she has done so, and feed back how mature she has been.

11. Write down family rules with which you all agree. Work these out together — you may all have to compromise — and all sign them. Stick to your side even if your child cannot.

12. When there are two parents, try to stick together and be consistent in your approach with your teenager, even if you are separated.

13. Whatever else is going on, make sure there are times when you talk to your son or daughter in a positive way. If they no longer accept hugs, then an arm round the shoulder for a few seconds, several times a day, gives the message that you care.

14. Rewarding your child for being less aggressive works better in the long run than punishing for being aggressive.

15. Remember, this is a team approach and your teenager may find it hard to change on his own.

Angela Hobday and Kate Ollier
From Ollier and Hobday (2001) *Creative Therapy 2: Working with Parents,* Impact Publishers, Inc.

Guidelines for Fathers to Assist Children in Split Families

Children often blame themselves — let them know it is not their fault.

Make sure you don't fight with your children's mother in the presence of your children.

When you have to say goodbye, let your children know of the next date and say "see you then."

Don't say things about your children's mother in front of them (bite your tongue).

Praise your children for their good behavior (visits are often a time for testing boundaries).

Let your children know that just because you don't love their mother as you used to, that has nothing to do with the way you love them, i.e., you still love your children just as much as before.

Let your children know that it is OK for them to love both their mother and their father.

If you have a partner, let your children know that they can still love their mother and your partner at the same time (love is not something that runs out).

If and when you tell off your children for doing something naughty, let them know that you are angry/upset about their *behavior*, not at them as people, and tell them you do love them.

Try to treat all your children equally regardless of parentage.

Respect appropriate rules, e.g., bedtimes, so that your children do not have to make big changes to their living patterns with each move.

Do keep your children informed of events — they miss out on much information by not always being with you.

Do not use your children as messengers between you and their mother.

Do not expect your children to keep secrets from their mother.

Help your children to express and cope with feelings of frustration and anger by encouraging talking and teaching appropriate ways of dealing with such feelings.

Kate Ollier and Angela Hobday
From Ollier and Hobday (2001) *Creative Therapy 2: Working with Parents,*
    Impact Publishers, Inc.

Guidelines for Mothers to Assist Children in Split Families

Children often blame themselves — let them know it is not their fault. Make sure you don't fight with your children's father in the presence of your children.

When you have to say goodbye, let your children know of the next date and say "see you then."

Don't say things about your children's father in front of them (bite your tongue).

Praise your children for their good behavior (visits are often a time for testing boundaries).

Let your children know that just because you don't love their father as you used to, that has nothing to do with the way you love them, i.e., you still love your children just as much as before.

Let your children know that it is OK for them to love both their mother and their father.

If you have a partner, let your children know that they can still love their father and your partner at the same time (love is not something that runs out).

If and when you tell off your children for doing something naughty, let them know that you are angry/upset about their *behavior*, not at them as people and tell them you do love them.

Try to treat all your children equally regardless of parentage.

Respect appropriate rules, e.g., bedtimes, so that your children do not have to make big changes to their living patterns with each move.

Do keep your children informed of events — they miss out on much information by not always being with you.

Do not use your children as messengers between you and their father.

Do not expect your children to keep secrets from their father.

Help your children to express and cope with feelings of frustration and anger by encouraging talking and teaching appropriate ways of dealing with such feelings.

Kate Ollier and Angela Hobday
From Ollier and Hobday (2001) *Creative Therapy 2: Working with Parents,*
Impact Publishers, Inc.

Helping Your Child to Become Less Anxious

An anxious child often has many symptoms; some common ones are:
- concentration problems
- memory problems
- distressed about a change in routine
- sleep problems
- eating problems
- low confidence in relationships and school work
- frequent headaches/stomach aches
- shyness and timidity
- nervousness/tension
- need for reassurance
- aggressive behavior in certain situations.

Your children may not have all of these symptoms, but here are some general guidelines that may be useful in helping them to become less stressed:

1. Always encourage your child
   - praise for small achievements
   - do not get angry if your child cannot do something
   - show your child how to do things he finds difficult
   - offer some help, but do not take over
   - avoid putting your child on the spot, she may not remember what you said or may be worried she'll get it wrong.

   Do not say "What did I tell you earlier?"
   Say instead "Do you remember me telling you about _____ earlier?"

2. Never confront your child
   He may find it more difficult to express himself next time. Do not use an angry voice, which may make your child more anxious.

   Instead... ask him questions clearly
   do not push your child beyond her limits

give reminders or hints to help your child
know how to do things
use an encouraging tone of voice.

3. Encourage friendships
Invite children to your home; do not expect an anxious child to do this on his own. If your child has been invited to a friend's house, encourage him to go, even for a short time. Always arrive to pick him up at the time promised.

4. Let your child talk

Your child may need to talk about fears. Some may seem like nothing to you but are very real to your child.

Do not focus only on difficulties. Help your child to tell you about good things that have happened as well.

Reward your child for talking to you and for any steps she has made towards overcoming her fears.

If your child talks about fears or problems, help him to think about ways to make things better.

5. Help your child to have times to relax
Some ways children relax are:
- quiet play
- listening to music
- watching a favorite video
- cuddling
- playing with pets.

Recognize that your child needs time to unwind, just as adults do.

6. Plan in advance
Let your child know what's coming in terms of outings, events and treats. Some children like to have their own calendar.

Remember:
Always praise and encourage your children; it will help to boost their confidence.

Angela Hobday and Kate Ollier
From Ollier and Hobday (2001) *Creative Therapy 2: Working with Parents,* Impact Publishers, Inc.

Appendix II-5

Helping Your Child to Feel Valued

Children who have been through difficult situations, or who have low self-esteem may think that they are not at all important. Here are some ways to help your child to feel special and valuable:

1. Think About How You Deal With Behavior
    Praise your child for good behavior. You may need to start noticing all the little things your child does right. Praise her for these and you will notice improvement in other ways.

    If you have to tell your child off, make it clear you don't like what he has done, but that you still love him.

    Never criticize your child in public. If your child has done something wrong, try to take her away from other people and explain gently why the behavior was wrong.

    Encourage your child's independence by giving him things to do that show you trust him. An example would be feeding your pet, or looking after something important.

    Never compare your child's behavior with others. If you tell your child that her behavior is not as good as someone else's, she may feel unimportant.

2. Take a Family View
    Try to treat all your children equally. This is especially important in step-families and foster families where children are of different parentage. However, it can be a problem in any family where one child seems less able or less confident than another. Older children will need some extra privileges and responsibilities, but it is important to make sure younger children understand they will have the same when they reach the right age.

    Family jokes and rituals need to be very positive. If nicknames are used these must be encouraging and suit the age of your child. Try not to use a nickname that emphasizes a part of the child that they see as a problem. For example, if a boy has red hair he may hate being called "Carrot-top" however lovingly it is said.

127

Never say your child will be sent away. No matter how bad the behavior is, this threat should never be used. The bad behavior itself may be because the child is worried about being sent away.

Ask your child's opinion on events, family matters, or the world! Show that you value what he says by listening and encouraging him to express his views.

Sort out family quarrels — do not just ignore them. Sometimes a more powerful sister or brother can undermine a child's feeling of being valued. Keep an eye on what is going on between your children and make sure everyone values each other.

Celebrate achievements — everyone's! Whether it is baby cutting her first tooth or Granddad finishing a crossword puzzle, there's usually something to celebrate if you look for it. Make sure you find things to celebrate for the child who needs to learn to feel valued, at least as often as everyone else.

3. Help Your Child to Talk to You
    Create the right mood. Have plenty of time when your child is not hungry or sleepy. If your child likes to cuddle, then it may help to put your arm around her as you talk. Sometimes children find it easier to talk while playing a game with you or while watching television together.

    Take your child seriously. Never laugh if your child tells you about a fear or problem. Reassure him if you think that the fear is something that he should not be worried about. If there is a real problem, talk to him about ways of overcoming it.

    Let your child draw or write feelings. Some children can draw angry or sad pictures. Others are better at writing their feelings down rather than talking about them directly to their parents.

    Reward your child and encourage them whenever she tries to tell you anything, or even sit and listen to you. A hug, a "Good job!" or other small reward will help her to feel valued.

    Show your child you understand. A useful phrase is "if something like that happened to me I would feel..."

Do not focus only on problems. When you are talking together, encourage your child to tell you about the good things that have happened. Write these down, so that you both remember them.

Angela Hobday, Anya Whitmarsh and Kate Ollier
From Ollier and Hobday (2001) *Creative Therapy 2: Working with Parents,* Impact Publishers, Inc.

Appendix II-6

Helping Your Child to Follow Requests

As children begin to grow up, it is normal for them to begin to challenge their parents. This is part of becoming more independent from you. However, it is important that your child learns to obey reasonable requests. If your child is refusing to obey you more often than following your requests, then it will help to follow these guidelines:

1. Give Children Attention When They Are Behaving As You Want Them To
   Giving attention is a very powerful reward for children. If your children get attention and praise for obeying you, then they are more likely to behave like that again. Always try to notice and praise your children for doing as they are told. For example, "I am very pleased with you for coming right away when I called you for dinner; good job."

2. Be Sure Your Request is Fair
   Think about the age and ability of your child and ask yourself whether your child is ready to understand or carry out your requests. If your child is not old enough to do the task on her own, you may have to offer to help before she will obey. For example, "Jenny, let's put away your toys together. I am putting your bricks in here like this. You do it now."

3. Always Be Very Clear About What You Want Your Child to Do, and When It Must Be Done
   Clear short sentences work much better than vague comments. For example, to say "Ryan, clean your room now, please" will get a better response than "Your room is always a mess. Why don't you ever clean it up?"

4. Tell Your Children What to Do, Don't Just Ask
   Children sometimes take things exactly as they sound. If you say "Will you come and sit at the table?" your child may think there is a choice and say "No." It is better to say "Jodie, please come and sit at the table now."

131

5. Be Polite and Keep Calm

   Children often "switch off" to shouting or angry voices. Your child is more likely to listen to you if you speak in a polite, clear manner.

6. Do Not Keep Repeating the Same Request

   If you find you have repeated your request more than twice, then it is likely your child has started to ignore you. Make sure your child is listening, by asking him to look at you, and tell him again. Make sure he understands what will happen if he does not obey. Also, remind him how pleased you will be when he does as he is told.

7. Do Not Make Weak or Foolish Threats

   Threats are very dangerous, so be very careful before you use them. If you make a threat you cannot carry out, your child will learn to ignore you. It is better to reward your child for good behavior so that loss of the reward is punishment enough.

   Withdrawing a special privilege is perhaps the only other acceptable threat. However, make sure you are not taking away something that will help your child. For example, do not stop her from going to Scouts if you know she is learning to behave better there. Always give your child a chance to change the behavior before punishing her.

8. Use Rewards

   You may wish to set up a system so that your child is rewarded for obeying you quickly. Star charts work well, backed up with little treats once your child has begun to earn some stars. Do not take the stars away once earned, or your child will give up on the rewards completely. Or you may wish to reward your child right away with extra time or attention. For example, say "Mary, please straighten your room now. When it is done we can sit down and have some milk and cookies together."

9. Ignore Bad Behavior

   Unless your child is hurting someone else or himself, ignore the bad behavior. Although he will be even worse for a while, he will learn that there are better ways of getting your attention. Remember to really praise your child when he is good.

10. Look Out for Bad Habits

Parents and children become stuck in patterns of behavior. Your child may be in the habit of saying "No" to you because she knows you will react in the same way each time. See if you can avoid letting her get into this pattern by not reacting. Just firmly state your request again, reminding her of the reward she will receive for obeying.

Angela Hobday and Kate Ollier
From Ollier and Hobday (2001) *Creative Therapy 2: Working with Parents,* Impact Publishers, Inc.

Helping the Child Who Worries Too Much

Some children worry about things more than others. They may get stomach aches or headaches because they are upset. Sometimes they act up because they are scared or worried. Here are some ways you can help your children not to worry so much:

1. Help your children feel good
   - Say "Good job!" even for little things they get right.
   - Give them some help with things they find hard.
   - Try not to get angry if they do things wrong.

2. Try not to argue with your children
   - Ask them about things in a calm tone of voice.
   - Try not to ask them to do things that are too hard for them.

3. Help your children to make new friends
   - Your child may be too shy to ask friends to the house. You may have to help with that.
   - If your child is asked out, and you are comfortable with the circumstances, tell her it would be good to go. Help her try to go for a little while.
   - Tell your child what time you will pick him up. Do not be late.

4. Let your children talk to you
   - Let them talk about good things as well as bad things.
   - Say "Good job!" to them for trying to talk.
   - When they have problems, help them to think of what to do.

5. Help your children to have quiet times to relax, for example:
   - Quiet play
   - Music
   - Watching a video
   - Having a hug
   - Playing with pets

6. Make plans
   - Let your child know what you are doing tomorrow or next week.

- Make a list of outings and special things that will happen.
- Help your child to write down the days these things will happen.

Remember:

Lots of hugs and saying "Good job!" will be the best help for your child.

Angela Hobday and Kate Ollier

From Ollier and Hobday (2001) *Creative Therapy 2: Working with Parents,* Impact Publishers, Inc.

❖

Sample Description of Clinical Services

CLINICAL PSYCHOLOGY
SERVICE TO CHILDREN AND ADOLESCENTS
KING'S LYNN AND WISBECH HOSPITALS NHS TRUST

INFORMATION LEAFLET

Dear Parent or Caregiver,

Your child has been referred to us and before you come we would like to tell you about our service. First, we would like you to know that it is a good decision to make an appointment to look at the problems you are having. We know that we see the parents who care the most about their children's welfare.

What is a Clinical Psychologist?
Child clinical psychologists work with children and young people and their families. They are specialists in the development and behavior of children and in child and adolescent psychology.

Clinical psychologists have a degree in psychology. They then work as a psychology assistant or in another job with people. After that they are trained for a further three years to get a higher degree in clinical psychology. During this training they usually begin to specialize in child psychology.

Which Psychologist Will My Child See?
The psychologist you see will depend on your child's difficulty. For example, one psychologist works with the Child Development Team with other therapists. Another psychologist has more experience with children in care.

Why Was My Child Referred?
Sometimes your child may have difficulties which seem to be physical. An example would be headaches. Your family doctor or pediatrician will have referred your child to see if there are any other reasons, like stress, which cause the problem. Or your child may have difficulties with feelings or behavior which we will be able to help you sort out. If there are concerns over the way your child is learning and developing, he or she may be coming for a developmental assessment.

What Will Happen at the First Appointment?

This will depend on the reason your child has been referred. Generally, at your first appointment you will be asked about things that may have happened to your child in the past, what happens now, and about the family generally. This will help you and your psychologist to understand the problem and to begin to work out together why it is there and what has kept it going. The length of this appointment is normally about one hour.

If your child has been referred for an assessment, this may take up to one-and-a-half hours and may need more than one visit. The aim is to find out what your child is good at and what he or she finds difficult. We try to make assessments fun, and use toys and puzzles. If your child wears glasses or a hearing aid, please make sure these are brought to the assessment.

Is My Child Seen Alone?

If your child is old enough, he or she will normally be asked to see the psychologist alone at some point. This will only be done if your child is happy to let you leave the room.

Will All the Family Be Seen Together?

The psychologist will usually want to see the referred child and parents/caregivers together for some of the sessions. At some stage, the psychologist may want to see the whole family, but this will be discussed with you. However, we do run a family clinic. You will receive separate information about this if you are to be seen in this clinic.

What About Confidentiality?

We treat the information you give us with the utmost confidentiality. We do not give private information about your child to schools, social services, or other agencies without asking your permission, unless we are required by law or to comply with local child protection guidelines.

A letter will go to the person who referred you to let him or her know what we are doing to resolve your child's problem. A copy is usually sent to your family doctor. If you are worried about confidentiality, please talk to us.

138

What Sort of Therapy Will Be Offered?
After your first visit you may be asked to provide more information about the problem. This will then be used by our psychologist and yourself to agree on the approach which best suits your child, yourself and the rest of your family. The psychologist will then work with you towards resolving the difficulty. The therapy will vary from talking things through, to working out practical strategies which you can use to resolve the problem. No therapy that can harm your child will be used. Psychologists do not prescribe medicines.

What Do I Tell My Child?
It is useful if you prepare your child for his or her visit. Please explain that the psychologist is there to help children and their families by talking and listening, playing and/or drawing. They will work out things you can do at home to help the problem go away. Please explain to your child that the psychologist sees lots of children who have very similar difficulties.

How Often Does My Child Have to See the Psychologist?
The number of appointments varies from one to several over a period of weeks or months. You will decide with the psychologist how often the appointments will be. Although the first appointment will probably be about one hour long, further appointments may be shorter. Usually we are only able to offer appointments between 9:00 a.m. and 5:00 p.m. on weekdays. Some psychologists work part time so can only offer particular days or times.

Does It Always Work?
We have a high success rate and we use a number of different methods and approaches. If the first treatment does not help to meet your need, we will be able to work out with you a change of approach. We will work together to find the best solution for your family. Sometimes we make referrals to a different agency.

Where Will We Be Seen?
Your appointment letter will tell you whether you should come to the Roxburgh Children's Center or the Clinical Psychology Department. Both are based

at the Queen Elizabeth Hospital, King's Lynn. Directions are in the referral letter.

I Do Not Think That My Child Needs to See a Psychologist Any More.
What Do I Do?

You may cancel the appointment by calling the contact number for your psychologist which is shown on the back of this leaflet, but please let us know if the problem is sorted out. However, if you think that this is only a temporary change or you still have concerns about your child, you are welcome to keep your appointment and talk this over with us. If you do cancel your appointment, please let us know as soon as possible, so that we can use the time for someone else.

Comments, Suggestions and Complaints

King's Lynn and Wisbech NHS Hospitals Trust recognizes that suggestions, ideas and complaints can be valuable in improving the services we offer. If you have any comments or complaints, please do not hesitate to contact:

(This section contains the names and address of the head of the Clinical Psychology Service to Children and Adolescents, and her immediate manager.)

We look forward to the time when you will meet one of us at the first appointment.

Best wishes

The Child and Adolescent Clinical Psychology Team

Names and Contact Numbers

(This section contains the name, qualifications, job title and phone number of each member of the team and his or her secretary.)

From Ollier and Hobday (2001) *Creative Therapy 2: Working with Parents,* Impact Publishers, Inc.

Appendix II-9

Reward Systems — Some Questions Answered

Why Rewards?

One of the best ways to help your child to behave better is to encourage behavior which is more acceptable. Most children respond well to rewards when they are learning new ways to behave. Rewards are not bribes, as they are not slipped to the child to perform a bad deed. A reward is something earned by working hard to behave well.

How Do Rewards Work?

Children who are having to change the way they behave are having to break a habit. This is hard work. It is easy to slip back if there is nothing to help them to remember and to keep alert enough to be able to change. Earning something as they progress will help your child to keep the new behavior going and to get rid of the bad behavior. Also, children who often behave badly generally have a poor opinion of themselves. Earning rewards helps them to see that they can achieve and not be told off all the time.

Can You Give Some Examples?

One example would be a boy who always throws a temper tantrum around bedtime. A reward can be offered for going to bed as soon as he is asked, with no problems.

An older child who is often grounded for having a messy room can instead be rewarded for straightening his bedroom once a week.

Will Rewards Work No Matter How They Are Given?

No. For a reward system to work, the following rules need to be remembered:

1. Once a reward is earned it must not be taken away, or the reward system will not work.

2. The child must know exactly what is required to achieve the reward, and this must not keep changing.

3. The reward must be given as soon as the good behavior has happened. This is very important for younger children, who will become confused if they are not rewarded immediately.

4. No other punishment, apart from no reward, should happen for that particular behavior (so never put black marks on a star chart).

5. The reward must be easy to earn, so do not make the goal too hard. It may be better to reward the child for a small step towards the required behavior.

6. As well as a reward like stars or money, it is important to praise your child.

7. Your child is learning a new way of behaving. This will take time so do not expect instant results.

8. It is better to start with one behavior rather than many different behaviors. Then both you and your child will be able to see progress.

9. Reward systems need to run for at least two weeks to find out if they are working.

10. If the system does not work at first, encourage and remind your child. Do not be angry with your child for not trying. Go for a smaller goal first.

What Are Record Sheets and Charts?
A record sheet is usually enjoyed by older children and is simply a way of noting whether or not they have achieved the goal. It can be a mark on a calendar or a note in a diary. It is usually better if the child can see the progress that is being made, so have the chart on a bulletin board or stuck up in the kitchen. However, do not put up the record where visitors can see it if the child is shy about the problem.

A star chart is similar but has space for the child to be awarded stars for the good behavior. Usually a space is needed for each day, but if the chart is for something that should happen several times a day, remember to allow for this when making the chart with the child.

What Sort of Rewards Should Be Used?
Star stickers are a form of reward in themselves, but usually need a bigger reward (e.g., a special pencil for three stars) to keep the chart going. Many parents have found that it works well to have a small selection of prizes which are chosen to please their child.

For example, in a tin or box for a boy there may be his favorite candy, sports stickers, a novelty pencil, ruler, a special key-chain and a quarter. He is allowed to choose an item out of the tin when he has reached a goal of three stars. After a while, when the behavior is easier, he may have to gain five stars for a reward.

Always link any reward with your praise. Eventually you will want your child to respond to your praise alone.

Finally . . . Try to make it fun! Spend time with your child making a chart and offering encouragement. Your child needs your help in changing his or her behavior, and rewarding can bring you both pleasure.

Angela Hobday and Kate Ollier
From Ollier and Hobday (2001) *Creative Therapy 2: Working with Parents*,
    Impact Publishers, Inc.

Ten Ways to Help Your Child to Talk to You

1. Create the right atmosphere
Have plenty of time when you and your child are not hungry or sleepy. If your child likes to cuddle, then it may help to put your arm round them as you talk.

2. Be prepared to listen
Your child may be trying to tell you something you do not expect to hear so be careful not to keep saying what you think is wrong.

3. Take your child seriously
Never laugh if children tell you about a fear or difficulty, but reassure them if you think it is something they should not be worried about.

4. Show your child that you understand
A useful phrase may be "if something like that happened to me I would feel…"

5. Play with your child as you talk
Many children cannot cope with a direct face-to-face conversation but can chatter while they play.

6. Tell them about feelings
Knowing that you have feelings too will help them if you think that they are holding back.

7. Use television programs
If a situation similar to your child's arises on the television try to discuss it with them without making it too obvious that you are discussing their own problems.

8. Use toys
With a younger child it is sometimes helpful to use toys to act out a situation. Or children sometimes find it easier to "tell Teddy" what is the matter. Puppets can be useful, too.

9. Let your child paint or write feelings

Some children can draw angry or sad pictures much more easily than talking. Talk about the pictures with them and tell them you understand how they are feeling.

10. Reward your child

Some children may need a hug, a "well done!" or other reward (like a sticker or small treat) just for listening at first. Older children may need a reward linked to whatever they have discussed with you, depending on the circumstances. For example, if they are upset because they feel left out, you may decide to spend some extra time with them doing something that is special to them.

Angela Hobday and Kate Ollier
From Ollier and Hobday (2001) *Creative Therapy 2: Working with Parents,*
    Impact Publishers, Inc.

When a Parent Goes Away

Children who are missing their parent will show several symptoms of grief. This can cause problems for the child. The problems are fairly similar whether the separation is because of a break-up in the marital relationship or for some other reason, e.g., because a parent is away working.

What Sort of Problems Are Likely to Develop?

Common problems may include any of the following:

Going backwards with skills already learned, e.g., eating, sleeping and toileting.

Anxiety — the child may become dependent or "clingy." They may have new fears, perhaps of the dark, and may lose trust in the remaining parent. **Poor behavior** at this time may be as a result of anxiety and trying to gain more attention.

Preoccupation with the absent parent may occur. Your child may constantly ask about the missing parent and what is happening.

Your child may have **fantasies** about the missing parent and about being totally abandoned, or both parents dying. This will lead to further anxiety and **fear.**

Sometimes children will also develop **physical problems,** like stomach aches or headaches. These are a result of the anxiety they feel.

What Can I Do to Help My Child?

The most important thing to do is to **listen** and **talk** with your child. Try to explain what is happening and why in the most simple way you can. If there are frightening details, e.g., if there is violence before a marriage break-up, it is not necessary to discuss this unless your child has witnessed it. **Show that you understand** how your children feel and explain that it is usual to feel how they do. Let them talk to you about their feelings and **listen** carefully.

Keep telling your children that **both parents still love them**, and that you are both still their parents, even though you are not together at the moment.

If the partner is coming back or visiting the child, explain this and put the **dates on the calendar** for the child to see. It may help to mark off the days as they pass.

Spend time with your children having fun together. Help your children to **relax**, especially at bedtime, so that they sleep well. With younger children **keep to your usual routine** as closely as possible.

Does My Child Need Extra Help?

You will need to seek professional help if your child still has difficulties which are not improving by three months after the separation. Seek help earlier if your child becomes severely depressed or talks about life being "not worth living."

Where Can I Find Help?

Talk to your doctor, who will refer you to a qualified professional who will work with you to help your child, or will give your child individual counseling, depending on his or her age.

Kate Ollier and Angela Hobday
From Ollier and Hobday (2001) *Creative Therapy 2: Working with Parents,*
    Impact Publishers, Inc.

Appendix III

Record Charts
❖

24-Hour Record Chart

Child's name _____ Recorded by _____

This is a record of _____

Date:						
Midnight – 1 am						
1 am – 2 am						
2 am – 3 am						
3 am – 4 am						
4 am – 5 am						
5 am – 6 am						
6 am – 7 am						
7 am – 8 am						
8 am – 9 am						
9 am – 10 am						
10 am – 11 am						
11 am – 12 noon						
12 noon – 1 pm						
1 pm – 2 pm						
2 pm – 3 pm						
3 pm – 4 pm						
4 pm – 5 pm						
5 pm – 6 pm						
6 pm – 7 pm						
7 pm – 8 pm						
8 pm – 9 pm						
9 pm – 10 pm						
10 pm – 11 pm						
11 pm – *Midnight*						

Please Record   Code

Behavior ....

Intensity ....

Other information ....

Kate Ollier and Angela Hobday (2001) *Creative Therapy 2: Working with Parents,* Impact Publishers, Inc.

ABC Record Chart

Child's name _____ Recorded by _____

This is a record of _____

Date	Time	**Antecedents** What happened before?	**Behavior** Describe the actual behavior	**Consequences** What happened next?

Kate Ollier and Angela Hobday (2001) *Creative Therapy 2: Working with Parents,* Impact Publishers, Inc.

Daytime Record Chart

Child's name _____   Recorded by _____

This is a record of _____

Date:							
Before 6 am							
6 am – 7 am							
7 am – 8 am							
8 am – 9 am							
9 am – 10 am							
10 am – 11 am							
11 am – 12 noon							
12 noon – 1 pm							
1 pm – 2 pm							
2 pm – 3 pm							
3 pm – 4 pm							
4 pm – 5 pm							
5 pm – 6 pm							
6 pm – 7 pm							
7 pm – 8 pm							
8 pm – 9 pm							
After 9 pm							

Please Record   Code

Behavior ....

Intensity ....

Other information ....

Kate Ollier and Angela Hobday (2001) *Creative Therapy 2: Working with Parents,* Impact Publishers, Inc.

Encouraging Change
Goal Sheet

After thinking about all areas of your child's welfare, and working out what must change for your child to change, see if you can work out barriers and small goals for change.

Barriers and Goals

1. Area _____
   Barrier _____
   Goal _____

2. Area _____
   Barrier _____
   Goal _____

3. Area _____
   Barrier _____
   Goal _____

4. Area _____
   Barrier _____
   Goal _____

5. Area _____
   Barrier _____
   Goal _____

Which of these areas can you or your family work on now?

Numbers _____

Who is responsible for beginning to work on the goals?

Number   **Person responsible**

_____   _____

_____   _____

_____   _____

Kate Ollier and Angela Hobday (2001) *Creative Therapy 2: Working with Parents,* Impact Publishers, Inc.

Appendix III-5

MY Record Chart

Name _____ Date _____

I am working on _____

My next step towards this is _____

I will get a star when _____

When I have _____ stars I can _____

Monday	Tuesday	Wednesday	Thursday	Friday	Saturday	Sunday

The problems I might have are _____

What I will do when I have problems is _____

Kate Ollier and Angela Hobday (2001) *Creative Therapy 2: Working with Parents,* Impact Publishers, Inc.

157

Appendix III-6

Parents Record Chart

Name _____ Date _____

This week we are working on:

My child will be rewarded when:

Please write down your child's progress and tick (　) if a reward was given

Monday	Tuesday	Wednesday	Thursday	Friday	Saturday	Sunday

Any problems? Don't give up! Write down what happend and we will try to sort it out.

Kate Ollier and Angela Hobday (2001) *Creative Therapy 2: Working with Parents,* Impact Publishers, Inc.

Requests Chart

What types of requests have we used with our child this week and what were the responses?

Date/Time	Type of Request	Example	Response

What have we noticed from the exercise?

_____

_____

_____

_____

_____

Kate Ollier and Angela Hobday (2001) *Creative Therapy 2: Working with Parents,* Impact Publishers, Inc.

Split-Day Record Chart

Child's name _____   Recorded by _____

This is a record of _____

Date	Morning	Afternoon	Evening

Kate Ollier and Angela Hobday (2001) *Creative Therapy 2: Working with Parents,* Impact Publishers, Inc.

Kate Ollier and Angela Hobday (2001) *Creative Therapy 2: Working with Parents,* Impact Publishers, Inc.

What Behaviors Can We Praise?

During this week, be very alert to anything that your child does which is a step in the right direction. Add these behaviors to your list as you spot them. If you remembered to praise them, indicate this on the sheet, by ticking. You may also wish to record if you did not have the opportunity to praise, or did not praise for any other reason.

Date/Time	Praiseworthy Behavior	Praised?	No Praise?

Have you noticed any changes in *a) yourself* or *b) your child* through doing this exercise? Please record below:

a) _____

b) _____

Kate Ollier and Angela Hobday (2001) *Creative Therapy 2: Working with Parents,* Impact Publishers, Inc.

References

Abidin, R. R. (1996). *Early Childhood Parenting Skills: A Program Manual for the Mental Health Professional.* Odessa, FL: Psychological Assessment Resources.

American Psychiatric Association (1994). *Diagnostic and Statistical Manual of Mental Disorders,* 4th ed. Washington: American Psychiatric Association.

Barker, P. (1995). *Basic Child Psychiatry,* 6th ed. Oxford: Blackwell Science Ltd.

Blechman, E. A. (1985). *Solving Child Behavior Problems — At Home and At School.* Champaign, IL: Research Press.

Bonner, B. L. and Everett, F. L. (1986). Influence of client preparation and problem severity on attitudes and expectations in psychotherapy. *Professional Psychology, Research and Practice,* 17, 223-229.

Burnham, J. B. (1988). *Family Therapy: First Steps Towards a Systemic Approach.* London: Routledge.

Cadranel J. (1991). Paediatrics. In H. Davies and L. Fallowfield (Eds) *Counseling and Communication in Health Care.* Chichester: Wiley.

Clarke-Stewart, K. A. (1998). Reading with children. *Journal of Applied Developmental Psychology,* 19(1), 1-14.

Cohen, D. A. and Rice, J. C. (1995). A parent-targeted intervention for adolescent substance use prevention: Lessons learned. *Evaluation Review,* 19(2), 159-180.

Crary, E. (1994). *Love & Limits: Guidance Tools for Creative Parenting.* Seattle, WA: Parenting Press.

D K Publishing (2000). *D K Merriam-Webster's Children's Dictionary.* New York: D K Publishing, Inc.

Dadds, M. R. (1992). Concurrent treatment of marital and child behaviour problems in behavioural family therapy. *Behaviour Change,* 9, 139-148.

Dadds, M. R. and Powell, M. B. (1991). The relationship of interparental conflict and global marital adjustment to aggression, anxiety, and immaturity in aggressive and nonclinic children. *Journal of Abnormal Child Psychology*, 19, 553-567.

Dadds, M. R., Sanders, M. R., Behrens, B. C. and James, J. E. (1987). Marital discord and child behavior problems: A description of family interactions during treatment. *Journal of Clinical Child Psychology*, 16(3), 192-203.

Davies, H. (1993). *Counseling Parents of Children with Chronic Illness or Disability*. Leicester: BPS Books (The British Psychological Society).

de Kemp, R. A. T. and Van Acker, J. C. A. (1997). Therapist-parent interaction patterns in home-based treatments: Exploring family therapy process. *Family Process*, 36, 281-295.

Dozier, R. M., Hicks, M. W., Cornille, T. A. and Peterson, G. W. (1998). The effect of Tomm's therapeutic questioning styles on therapeutic alliance: A clinical analog study. *Family Process*, 37, 189-200.

D'Zurilla, T. J. and Nezu, A. (1982). Social problem-solving in adults. In P. C. Kendall (Ed.) *Advances in Cognitive-Behavioral Research and Therapy* (Vol. 1). New York: Academic Press.

Elias, M. J., Tobias, S. E., Friedlander, B., and Chopra, G. (2000). *Raising Emotionally Intelligent Teenagers: Parenting with Love, Laughter, and Limits*. New York: Harmony Books.

Fahlberg, V. I. (1994). *A Child's Journey Through Placement* (UK ed.). London: British Agencies for Adoption and Fostering.

Forehand, R., Lautenschlager, G. J., Faust, J. and Graziano, W. G. (1986). Parent perceptions and parent-child interactions in clinic-referred children: A preliminary investigation of the effects of maternal depressive moods. *Behaviour, Research and Therapy*, 24(1), 73-75.

Forgatch, M. S. and Patterson, G. R. (1989). *Parents and Adolescents Living Together* Vol. 2, Family Problem-solving. Eugene, OR: Castalia.

Freeman, K. A., Adams, C.D. and Drabman, R. S. (1998). Divorcing parents: Guidelines for promoting children's adjustment. *Child and Family Behavior Therapy*, 20(3), 1-27.

Geldard, K. and Geldard, D. (1997). *Counseling Children*. London: Sage Publications.

Goldfarb, J. (1998). A physician's perspective on dealing with cases of Munchausen by proxy. *Clinical Pediatrics*, 37(3), 187-189.

Gowers, E. (1973). *The Complete Plain Words,* Rev. ed. London: Penguin.

Green, C. (1999). *Taming Toddlers.* New York: Fawcett Books

Green, J. M. and Murton, F. E. (1993). *Duchenne Muscular Dystrophy: The Experience of 158 Families.* Cambridge: Centre for Family Research.

Green, R. J. and Herget, M. (1991). Outcomes of systemic/strategic team consultation: III. The importance of therapist warmth and active structuring. *Family Process,* 30(3), 321-336.

Gross, A. M., Johnson, T. C., Wojnilower, D. A. and Drabman, R. S. (1985). The relationship between sports fitness training and social status in children. *Behavioral Engineering,* 9(2), 58-65.

Groth-Marnat, G. (1990). *Handbook of Psychological Assessment,* 2nd ed. New York: John Wiley and Sons.

Halford, W. K. and Sanders, M. R. (1989). Behavioural marital therapy in the treatment of psychological disorders. *Behaviour Change,* 6, 165-177.

Hampson, R. B. and Beavers, W. R. (1996). Family therapy and outcome: Relationships between therapist and family styles. *Contemporary Family Therapy,* 18(3), 345-370.

Harrison, S. and Bakker, P. (1998). Two new readability predictors for the professional writer: Pilot trials. *Journal of Research in Reading,* 21(2), 121-138.

Herbert, M. (1987). *Behavioural Treatment of Children with Problems: A Practice Manual.* London: Academic Press.

Herbert, M. (1991). *Clinical Child Psychology: Social Learning, Development and Behaviour.* Chichester: Wiley.

Herbert, M. (1996a). *ABC of Behavioural Methods. Parent, Adolescent and Child Training Series (PACTS).* Leicester: BPS Books (The British Psychological Society).

Herbert, M. (1996b). *Parent, Adolescent and Child Training Series (PACTS).* Leicester: BPS Books (The British Psychological Society).

Hobday, A. and Lee, K. (1995). Adoption: A specialist area for psychology? *The Psychologist,* 8(1), 13-15.

Hobday, A. and Ollier, K. (1999). *Creative Therapy: Activities with Children and Adolescents.* Atascadero, CA: Impact Publishers, Inc.

Hughes, Daniel A. (1999). *Building the Bonds of Attachment: Awakening Love in Deeply Troubled Children.* New York: Jason Aronson.

Iannotti, R. J., Cummings, E. M., Pierrehumbert, B., Milano, M. J. and Zahn-Waxler, C. (1992). Parental influences on prosocial behavior and empathy in early childhood.

In J. M. A. M. Janssens and J. R. M. Gerris (Eds) *Child Rearing: Influence on Prosocial and Moral Development*. Amsterdam: Swets and Zeitlinger.

Jones, D. N., Pickett, J., Oates, M. R. and Barker, P. (1987). *Understanding Child Abuse*. London: Macmillan.

Kirk, J. (1989). Cognitive-behavioural assessment. In K. Hawton, P. M. Salkovskis, J. Kirk and D. M. Clark (Eds) *Cognitive Behaviour Therapy for Psychiatric Problems*. Oxford: Oxford University Press.

Klein, J. D. (1997). National longitudinal study on adolescent health. Preliminary results: Great expectations. *Journal of the American Medical Association*, 278, 864-865.

Kottler, J. A. and Brown, R. W. (1985). *Introduction to Therapeutic Counseling*. Pacific Grove, CA: Brooks/Cole Publishing.

La Greca, A. M. (1983). Interviewing and behavioral observations. In C. E. Walker and M. C. Roberts (Eds) *Handbook of Clinical Child Psychology*. New York: Wiley.

Lask, B. and Bryant-Waugh, R. (1993). *Childhood Onset Anorexia Nervosa and Related Eating Disorders*. Hove: Psychology Press.

Le Bas, J. (1989). Comprehensibility of patient education literature. *Australian and New Zealand Journal of Psychiatry*, 23(4), 542-546.

Lefcourt, H. M. (1976). *Locus of Control*. Hillsdale, NJ: Erlbaum.

Ley, P. (1973). The measurement of comprehensibility. *Journal of the Institute of Health Education*, 11, 17-20.

Marcus, A., Ammermann, C., Klein, M. and Schmidt, M. H. (1995). Munchausen syndrome by proxy and factitious illness: Symptomatology, parent-child interaction, and psychopathology of the parents. *European Child and Adolescent Psychiatry*, 4(4), 229-236.

Mash, E. J. and Johnston, C. (1990). Determinants of parenting stress: Illustrations from families of hyperactive children and families of physically abused children. *Journal of Clinical Child Psychology*, 19(4), 313-328.

McColloch, M. A., Gilbert, D. G. and Johnson, S. (1990). Effects of situational variables on the interpersonal behavior of families with an aggressive adolescent. *Personality and Individual Differences*, 11, 1-11.

McGoldrick, M., Giordano, J. and Pearce, J. K. (Eds) (1996). *Ethnicity and Family Therapy,* 2nd ed. London: Guilford Press.

Meade, C. D. and Smith, C. F. (1991). Readability formulas: Cautions and criteria. *Patient Education and Counseling,* 17(2), 153-158.

Montgomery, B. and Morris, L. (1988). *Getting on With Your Teenagers.* Lothian: Melbourne.

Morrison, J. (1995). *The First Interview: Revised for DSM-IV.* London: Guilford Press.

Newby, R. F. (1996). Parent training for children with attention-deficit/hyperactivity disorder. In (No authorship indicated) *The Hatherleigh Guide to Psychiatric Disorders. The Hatherleigh Guides Series.* New York: Hatherleigh Press.

Parnell, T. F. and Day, D. O. (1998). *Munchausen by Proxy Syndrome: Misunderstood Child Abuse.* Thousand Oaks, CA: Sage Publications.

Peterson, B. T., Clancy, S. J., Champion, K. and McLarty, J. W. (1992). Improving readability of consent forms: What the computers may not tell you. *Irb: A Review of Human Subjects Research,* 14(6), 6-8.

Pilkonis, P. A., Imber, S. D., Lewis, P. and Rubinsky, P. (1984). A comparative outcome study of individual, group and conjoint psychotherapy. *Archives of General Psychiatry,* 41, 431-437.

Putallaz, M. and Heflin, A. H. (1990). Parent-child interaction. In S. R. Asher and J. D. Coie (Eds) *Peer Rejection in Childhood.* Cambridge: Cambridge University Press.

Reed, J., Conneely, J., Gorham, P. and Coxhead, S. (1993). Assessing the written information given to families prior to their attendance at a child development centre. *Child: Care, Health and Development,* 19(5) 317-325.

Rober, P. (1998). Reflections on ways to create a safe therapeutic culture for children in family therapy. *Family Process,* 37, 201-213.

Rueter, M. A. and Conger, R. D. (1995). Interaction style, problem-solving behavior, and family problem-solving effectiveness. *Child Development,* 66, 98-115.

Ryle, A. (1990). *Cognitive-Analytic Therapy: Active Participation in Change. A New Integration in Brief Psychotherapy.* Chichester: Wiley.

Sanders, M. R. and Dadds, M. R. (1993). *Behavioral Family Intervention.* Boston: Allyn and Bacon.

Sanders, M. R., Turner, K. M. T, and Markie-Dadds, C. (1996a). *Positive Parenting: A Guide to Children's Behaviour.* Brisbane: Families International.

Sanders, M. R., Turner, K. M. T. and Markie-Dadds, C. (1996b). *Positive Parenting of Preschool Children.* Brisbane: Families International.

Sanders, M. R., Turner, K. M. T. and Markie-Dadds, C. (1996c). *Positive Parenting of Infants and Toddlers.* Brisbane: Families International.

Sanders, M. R., Turner, K. M. T. and Markie-Dadds, C. (1996d). *Positive Parenting of Primary School Children.* Brisbane: Families International.

Sanders, M. R., Morrison, M., Rebgetz, M., Bor, W., Dadds, M. and Shepherd, R. (1990). Behavioural treatment of childhood recurrent abdominal pain: Relationships between pain, children's psychological characteristics and family functioning. *Behaviour Change, 7,* 16-24.

Sarason, B. R., Shearin, E. N., Pierce, G. R. and Sarason, I. G. (1987). Interrelations of social support measures: Theoretical and practical implications. *Journal of Personality and Social Psychology,* 52(4), 813-832.

Sattler, J. M. (1988). *Assessment of Children,* 3rd ed. San Diego: Jerome M. Sattler.

Sawyer, M. H. (1991). A review of research in revising instructional text. *Journal of Reading Behavior,* 23(3), 307-333.

Seligman, L. (1990). *Selecting Effective Treatments.* Oxford: Jossey-Bass Publishers.

Seligman, M. E. P. (1992). *Learned Optimism.* Sydney: Random House.

Shumow, L. (1998). Promoting parental attunement to children's mathematical reasoning through parent education. *Journal of Applied Developmental Psychology,* 19(1), 109-127.

Singh, J. (1995). The readability of educational materials written for parents of children with attention-deficit hyperactivity disorder. *Journal of Child and Family Studies,* 4(2), 207-218.

Spivack, G., Platt, J. J. and Shure, M. B. (1976). *The Problem-solving Approach to Adjustment.* London: Jossey-Bass Publishers.

Stein, H. T. (1991). Classical Alderian psychotherapy: A Socratic approach. *Individual Psychology: Journal of Alderian Theory, Research and Practice,* 47(2), 241-246.

Strupp, H. H. (1981). Toward the refinement of time-limited dynamic psychotherapy. In S. H. Budman (Ed.) *Forms of Brief Therapy*. New York: Guilford Press.

Thoits, P. A. (1986). Social support as coping assistance. *Journal of Consulting and Clinical Psychology*, 54(4), 416-423.

Warr, M. (1993). Parents, peers and delinquency. *Social Forces*, 72(1), 247-264.

Webster-Stratton, C. (1990). Stress: A potential disruptor of parents' perceptions and family interactions. *Journal of Clinical Child Psychology*, 19(4), 302-312.

Webster-Stratton, C. (1992a). *The Incredible Years: A Trouble-Shooting Guide for Parents of Children Aged 3-8*. Ontario: Umbrella Press.

Webster-Stratton, C. (1992b). *The Parents and Children Series*. No place indicated: Webster-Stratton.

Webster-Stratton, C. (1994). Using videotape parent training: A comparison study. *Journal of Consulting and Clinical Psychology*, 62, 583-593.

Webster-Stratton, C. (1998). Preventing conduct problems in Head Start children: Strengthening parenting competencies. *Journal of Consulting and Clinical Psychology*, 66(5), 715-730.

Wolfe, D. A. (1987). *Child Abuse: Implications for Child Development and Psychopathology*. Thousand Oaks, CA: Sage.

Wolff, S. (1996). Child psychotherapy. In S. Bloch (Ed.) *An Introduction to the Therapies*, 3rd ed. Oxford: Oxford University Press.

Young, I. L., Anderson, C. and Steinbrecher, A. (1995). Unmasking the phantom: Creative assessment of the adolescent. *Psychotherapy*, 32 (1), 34-38.

Zuckerman, E. L. (1993). *The Clinician's Thesaurus*, 3rd ed. Pittsburgh, PA: The Clinician's Tool Box.

Index

The Practical Therapist Series®

Books in *The Practical Therapist Series* are designed to answer the troubling "what-do-I-do-now-and-how-do-I-do-it?" questions often confronted in the practice of psychotherapy. Written in plain language, technically innovative, theoretically integrative, filled with case examples, *The Practical Therapist Series*® brings the wisdom and experience of expert mentors to the desk of every therapist.

Creative Therapy with Children and Adolescents

Angela Hobday, M.Sc., and Kate Ollier, M.Psych.
Hardcover: $21.95   192 pages   ISBN: 1-886230-19-6
Over 100 activities for therapeutic work with children, adolescents, and families. Simple ideas, fun games, fresh innovations to use as tools to supplement a variety of therapeutic interventions.

Integrative Brief Therapy
Cognitive, Psychodynamic, Humanistic & Neurobehavioral Approaches
John Preston, Psy.D.
Hardcover: $~~27.95~~ $17.95 272 pages ISBN: 1-886230-09-9
Answers the perennial therapist question, "What do I do now?" Integrates proven elements of therapeutic efficacy from diverse theoretical viewpoints. *(Discounted due to minor printer errors. Text is complete and perfectly readable.)*

Meditative Therapy
Facilitating Inner-Directed Healing
Michael L. Emmons, Ph.D.
Softcover: $27.95   230 pages   ISBN: 1-886230-11-0
Guide to creating the conditions for natural healing and recovery. Help clients harness their inner resources for emotional, physical, and spiritual growth.

Rational Emotive Behavior Therapy
A Therapist's Guide
Albert Ellis, Ph.D., and Catharine MacLaren, M.S.W., CEAP
Hardcover: $24.95   176 pages   ISBN: 1-886230-12-9
Up-to-date guidebook by the innovator of Rational Emotive Behavior Therapy. Includes thorough description of REBT theory and procedures, case examples, exercises.

Please see the following page for more books.